MONSTROUS WORK AND
RADICAL SATISFACTION

Monstrous Work and Radical Satisfaction

Black Women Writing under Segregation

Eve Dunbar

University of Minnesota Press
Minneapolis
London

The University of Minnesota Press gratefully acknowledges the generous assistance provided for the publication of this book by Vassar College.

A portion of chapter 4 was previously published in a different form as "Loving Gorillas: Segregation Literature, Animality, and Black Liberation," *American Literature* 92, no. 1 (March 2020): 123–49. Copyright 2020 Duke University Press. All rights reserved. Reprinted by permission of the publisher, https:// dukepress.edu.

Published by the University of Minnesota Press
111 Third Avenue South, Suite 290
Minneapolis, MN 55401-2520
http://www.upress.umn.edu

ISBN 978-1-5179-1786-9 (hc)
ISBN 978-1-5179-1787-6 (pb)

A Cataloging-in-Publication record for this book is available from the Library of Congress.

Printed in the United States of America on acid-free paper

The University of Minnesota is an equal-opportunity educator and employer.

UMP BmB 2024

Contents

Preface

As a child with a dead mother, I spent a good bit of my adolescence pretending my mother was not dead. I would insist to my classmates in my predominantly white high school that they only ever saw me in my grandparents' company because my mother was just too busy working to attend school-related events. Of course, there is the trauma reading, which I will not deny you. But trauma cannot account for a whole life, so I will tangle with the historical and the systemic. The social expectations that dictate respectability and the correct comportment of Black people in public is a part of this book's overarching story. Black comportment promises social legitimacy if carried out correctly, or so the myth foretells. Thus, the mother of my mind was an "always-working Black mother" because I sought not just to mend my emotional loss but also to conform to our society's expectation of productivity from its Black citizens—dead or alive. We were always only ever perceived as useful bodies that labor, working harder than expected and as close to uncompensated as possible.

During her short adulthood, my mother worked briefly as an administrative assistant in downtown Hartford, Connecticut. She sold summer sausages in the suburban mall during the winter holiday season. My mother once got paid to walk a runway for her boyfriend's fly-by-night fashion show business—she was only 5′4″ tall, and his self-disclosed claim to fame was that he had been gonged off the *Gong Show* for his singing.[1] I suspect my mother had many other odd jobs.

Still, most of the time, my mother's only work was to take care of her three children, which she did with the support of public assistance. She spent little of the decade that would constitute her adulthood working consistently or "productively." Instead, she gave birth for the first time at nineteen, shortly after graduating from high school, and died unexpectedly a few months before her thirtieth year, leaving in the wake three children between the ages of two and ten years old. In this way, my mother fits many statistics about Blackness, womanhood, poverty and precarity, educational access, and all the other things to which one falls prey or overcomes as a Black woman in the United States.

Soon after their youngest daughter died, my grandparents found themselves facing another loss: the shuttering of the tannery where my grandfather had spent most of his working life. My grandfather met my grandmother while stationed in South Carolina in the latter days of World War II. After the war ended, my grandparents married and moved to raise their family in New Hampshire, my grandfather's home state.

For her part, my grandmother left her family's land—which they had worked since before emancipation, first as enslaved laborers, and then as supposedly free sharecroppers—to become part of the Second Great Migration. She overshot D.C., Philadelphia, and New York City by a few hundred miles and settled in New England with flair. Every time I encounter Dorothy West's Cleo Judson, I think of my grandmother's trek from South Carolina and her unmistakable beauty; I remember stories that illustrated her conflicted love of the American South and less-than-fond memories of growing up "down there," under segregation.[2] I see my grandmother, clad head to toe in fur walking into the sanctuaries of all-white Episcopal churches. In my vision, my grandmother sticks out like a sore thumb not merely because of the brownness of her skin but because the context deformed her mode of self-presentation, which she meant to represent her family's success and right to (spiritual) life. Fur coats mean something to working-class Black women of a particular generation.

By the early 1950s, my grandfather, having returned to New Hampshire with his new family, took up his life's work. Maybe because he could pass as white, perhaps because he was a local, probably because he was a man in the United States, likely some combination of all, he secured stable work in one of the tanneries dotting the Merrimack River. He worked in leather processing plants for nearly four decades, slowly moving up the ranks in his labor union and supervising his line, which mixed the dangerous chemicals needed to strip cow hair off the hides to ready them for tanning. My grandmother worked less stable, nonunionized textile and mechanical factory jobs throughout those decades, bearing and rearing four children along the way.

If you could have heard my grandparents talk at night over oven-fried hamburgers or salmon croquettes and mashed potatoes, you would know that factory work was hard and dangerous, but good, work. It paid reasonably well if you pulled your weight, and my grandparents always pulled their weight. They lived what was a fairy-tale for Black folks of a particular generation: steady work with a pension promised at the end of it all. They raised four children, paid for their home, had a car and a television. They lived a version of the American Dream.

Until they did not.

Like many blue-collar workers of all races and genders laboring in industrialized northeastern cities in the late twentieth century, my grandparents were caught up in slowly expiring industries. Globalization and mandates from the U.S. Environmental Protection Agency to protect and preserve the Merrimack River conspired to make tanning leather and constructing small mechanical products less profitable. And as the tanning industry began to fail, my grandparents left their home of over thirty years to move with the plant down to more friendly environs: rural Pennsylvania in the mid-1980s. Perhaps because there were creeks there, not rivers, factory owners saw hope and promised their employees continued opportunity. At this next factory, working families that had been able to migrate deluded themselves into thinking this factory would succeed in escaping the shuttered fate of the previous one. It did not. By the late 1980s, my grandfather was forcibly retired from an occupation that now barely exists in the United States except as an artisanal pastime.

I write this not as a lamentation for a dying industry. I do not seek to resurrect death-bound industries simply because they fed my family for a few generations. And the ecological damage wrought by unregulated industry continues to affect the health and living conditions of many Black members of the working class and nonworking people in the United States. I want to work against nostalgic thinking, opting instead to return to the Black past to find ways of imagining Black being beyond the customary bounds of liberal democratic inclusion in a dream, the American Dream, that fails so many. The looming climate apocalypse requires at least this little from each of us.

It has taken me a lifetime of reading and reeducation to see and recognize what I will call (and argue for) throughout this book "monstrous work": the work of Black people for Black people, work that attempts to foster and provide healthy choices, second chances, access to futures.[3] Caring for the lives and living of Black people has never been legitimate in the eyes of the state, though it is some of the most challenging work. We see this on the national stage as we remember Trayvon, Tamir, Michael, Eric, Cynthia, Carole, Addie Mae, Denise, and all the other Black people who are no longer here but will always be somebody's baby. My idea of monstrous work is meant to sit alongside what Christina Sharpe calls "wake work," or "the plotting, mapping, and collecting the archives of every day of Black immanent and imminent death, and in the tracking the ways we resist rupture, disrupt that immanence and imminence aesthetically and materially."[4]

My project in this book, then, is to capture the radical work of satisfaction that Black women, in particular, have imagined during the same period my grandparents worked and raised their family. Because work and an idealized relationship to the American Dream of access and inclusion weigh so heavily in my family history, in this book I wanted to think along with narratives that place an emphasis on the materiality of Black women's caring and caregiving. The capaciousness of Black imagination in crafting other ways of relating to the promise of national inclusion is at the center of this project. Monstrous work and radical satisfaction orient, guide, and nurture in this book.

The Radical Satisfaction of
Black Women's Monstrous Work

In an August 11, 1955, letter to the editor of the Orlando *Sentinel*, a bit over a year after the May 17, 1954, Supreme Court decision in *Brown vs. Board of Education of Topeka*, writer Zora Neale Hurston proposes that desegregation might be nothing more than a political ruse, that the end of segregation "is not here and never meant to be here at present."[1] She stipulates that rather than relishing integration, she seeks to tend to the questions of "self-respect" and "race pride" for Black people.[2] In the letter to the editor, Hurston's critique of integration seems to center on the government's failure to undo the anti-Black racism that has historically undergirded the nation's ethos, justifying de facto and de jure forms of segregation.

Under Hurston's scrutiny, desegregation seeks to signal progress where there is none. Then, as now, the nation had yet to encounter or undo its commitment to white supremacy. Moreover, Hurston resists the false promises of integration as racial reconciliation and progress, with its inherent assumptions of Black deficiency, as proximity to whiteness and white people. In the published letter, Hurston appears to understand that a system designed to ensure Black dehumanization could not be trusted to recognize Black life and work.

That said, Hurston's critique of integration was misunderstood in her time by both white segregationists and civil rights leaders. For instance, interspersed in Hurston's papers in the University of Florida Archives are letters from white segregationists and members of Citizens' Council groups agreeing with Hurston's refusal of integration, commending her thinking, and asking her if they might reprint her letter for their members. Likewise, Hurston was dreadfully out of step with the ideological stance of the National Association for the Advancement of Colored People (NAACP), which supported

Brown's premise that the deep psychological injuries inflicted on Black children under segregation could only be remedied through legislated racial integration. The NAACP found it difficult to reconcile rhetorical resistance against *Brown* with its progressive democratic ideology.[3] Finally, many scholars analyzing Hurston's work and political conservativism "rob Hurston of any political awareness and astuteness and render her an overly emotional, irrational nonintellectual," according to Deborah G. Plant.[4] Many painted her as inconsistent and ignorant in her conservatism; yet Hurston writes, "I can see no tragedy in being too dark to be invited to a white school social affair. The Supreme Court would have pleased me more if they had concerned themselves about enforcing the compulsory education provisions for Negroes in the South as is done for white children."[5] I understand the misapprehensions that have grown around Hurston's criticism of *Brown* as illustrative of the illegibility of Black women writers and thinkers when they turn away from the empty promises of a nation bent on inclusion without revision.

Hurston's 1955 rejection of desegregation prompts me to question the nature and modes of satisfaction the United States sought to make available to Black people in the Jim Crow era. I am additionally compelled to ask and attempt to answer what it might mean to read Black women's segregation literature not for the wounds segregation inflicted on the psyches of African Americans or how it shaped the narratives of Black writing about integration toward integrationist concerns but for the ways writers model satisfaction and self-regard in the midst of a nation that could not care less for Black health and life. In the face of liberal democratic values, Hurston places an implicit value on Black life and epistemological production outside of what the state proffers. Proximity to whiteness does not augment Hurston's commitment to writing from and for Black worth, particularly Black Southern worth. From the vantage of the twenty-first century, it appears that there was little authentic satisfaction or restoration of wholeness for Black people: in 2022 the U.S. Government Accountability Office reported to Congress that one-third (about 18.5 million) of all schoolchildren attend predominantly same-race/ethnicity schools.[6] Hurston seemed to understand in 1955 the limits of the national imagination and of its legislative, juridical, and ideological mechanisms in supporting the lives of African Americans.

Building off the spirit of Hurston's critique of integration in the 1955 letter to the editor, *Monstrous Work and Radical Satisfaction* explores Black women's writing both in excess of and against modes of national belonging as the nation transitioned from the Jim Crow to the integrationist era. I extend Hurston's observations about Black worth regardless of its proximity to whiteness to theorize and emphasize the many contours of satisfaction in the writings of Ann Petry, Dorothy West, Alice Childress, and Gwendolyn Brooks. Moreover, I explore how these writers distinguish satisfaction from capitulation to the state-sanctioned forms of liberal integration—meant to serve as evidence of national racial progress—that were developing during the decades these writers published. Racial integration may satisfy the nation, but it has not historically met the long-term needs of Black people's quest for equity (or reparations) in the United States. My interest in tracking Black dissatisfaction within the nation motivates my analytical emphasis on literary moments of disruption, miscommunication, or confusion rather than ease, assimilation, and mutual understanding around race and gender.

In other words, Black satisfaction takes the place of proving that Black people are "humans too" or "worthy" of American citizenship to some imagined audience invested in a kind of liberal integration that requires assimilation. Such a desire for assimilation simply replicates the fallacy of liberal humanism's pluralism, which extends the umbrella of rights to marginalized groups without ever deconstructing the practices of exclusion. Incorporation is not equity. Instead, an animating premise of my work is the belief that these writers and the works they produced preternaturally understood that the promise of segregation's end would not repair or redress what has been stolen from or the violence against Black people in the United States. So, in contrast to reading the Jim Crow period simply for the racial and gender injury it produces, I examine literary representations of what I call "radical satisfaction": how texts explore examples of Black women's completeness, joy, and happiness outside the bounds of normative racial inclusion.

Monstrous Work and Radical Satisfaction is a project haunted by the contemporary racial landscape of the United States—the racial reckoning of Black Lives Matter and the uprisings of 2020—though it is focused on literature written decades earlier, in a different moment of racial crisis. The haunting of the now has only become more acute living with the Covid-19 pandemic and watching the United States encounter and deny its history of encouraging Black death, or what Christina Sharpe calls living in "the wake."[7] Amid all this death and social uprising, I have been thinking and writing about what it might mean to do "good work" within the university setting for a number of years now. Likewise, the constant national racial upheaval of the twenty-first century finds me worrying over how one works within any American institution founded on, at best, the benign neglect of Black people. To continue to do the work I seek to do within the confines of the university, I have had to lean into the idea of refusing inclusion, a practice of acting (what I call) "monstrous," which I will define more fully later in this introduction. The original title for this book was simply *Monstrous Work*, because, at the time I began the project, I needed to think into the boldness, endangerment, loss, and possibility of what it might mean to be a Black woman who refuses to center and do the work of whiteness. What happens to the Black woman who refuses the potential upward mobility (financial, professional, social) offered by liberal inclusion? It felt monstrous to imagine, and so I began looking for "monstrousness" in the works I read.

Yet, in the process of writing, I realized what I was tracking was not merely the monstrosity of not desiring to be included but the satisfaction that becomes central when one is working not for inclusion or integration but toward some more personal goal that will, in fact, make inclusion less possible.[8] In this way, satisfaction is akin to what Tina M. Campt calls "refusal": those practices that "undermine, disrupt, or destabilize the logic of the dominant."[9] For my work, more than mere disruption of the dominant, I am interested in marking the affective narrative possibilities in which Black women find shelter and support and some semblance of wholeness. I discuss these possibilities as evidence of radical satisfaction in this text. Satisfaction is aligned with completion, with having one's needs met and desires fulfilled.

Monstrous Work and Radical Satisfaction focuses on the writings of Ann Petry, Dorothy West, Alice Childress, and Gwendolyn Brooks in order to pick up and continue the work that has been done on the segregation era's influence on, and modeling of, Black artistic production—and further, and most importantly, to show how mid-century Black women writers insisted upon satisfaction and not merely survival. Focusing on roughly the same period and mentioning many of the same writers, in *The Indignant Generation: A Narrative History of African American Writers and Critics, 1934–1960*, Lawrence P. Jackson traces how both men and women writers of the midcentury harnessed what he describes as their "indignation at Jim Crow" to produce a new era of "psychological freedom" for African Americans.[10] His work is a grand historical overview of a literary movement, as his title suggests, that seeks to take account of literary influence and networks that produced the writing of the midcentury as a recognizable and collective project. While I am interested in the larger critical movement of the midcentury, I believe a more focused exploration of the women writing during these decades reveals particular relationships to Blackness, nation, and integration.

Toward particularity, I pay special attention not just to these authors' take on work and laboring but also to small things often overlooked in literary studies of mid-twentieth-century African American women writers' radicalism: child-rearing, cooking and eating, sleeping and dreaming, and friendship. And I treat these more mundane acts as aesthetic articulations of radicalism that are just as important as traditionally paid labor and labor activism. Focusing on the domestic, the interpersonal, and the small acts of refusal initiated in the works of Petry, West, Childress, and Brooks allows me to develop and reorient the eye toward the ways segregation-era women's writing shifts perspectives on what possibilities lie beyond racial integration and how those possibilities might register satisfaction in monstrous and productive ways.

Satisfaction and Monstrous Turns

What do I mean when I suggest that one might read for satisfaction in Black women's midcentury texts? Or how am I determining when a text delves into the realm of satisfaction? At some level, the answers to these questions are elusive because satisfaction is subjective, a deeply personal feeling. Each person experiences satisfaction in their own way: the first bite of one's favorite food cooked by a beloved aunt, the touch of a lover's or one's own hand, the end of a workday, the smile of a child, a stretch that releases the lower back, the list can go on and on in terms of what a person might find satisfying.

Yet, we should not be surprised to learn that there is a five-question psychological instrument meant to measure the feeling called the Satisfaction with Life Scale. Developed in the 1980s, this scale attempts to quantify the ephemeral by asking questions meant to assess "global life satisfaction."[11] This self-assessment tool offers an allegedly scientific accounting of satisfaction. However, in this book, I do not seek to quantify or create a taxonomy of satisfaction. Instead, I lean into the ways in which writers attempt to register what brings their Black women characters joy or fullness in their life experiences as Black people. What aligns my textual explorations, then, is an attention to representations of a sense of completion or of having one's needs and desires fulfilled. More important is my assertion that these Black characters' quests for forms of completion or wholeness often exist outside the national project of integration, which promised proximity to whiteness but not wholesale racial redress or an end to racial terror.

Audre Lorde's canonical essay "Uses of the Erotic: The Erotic as Power" offers some insight into how Black feminists have theorized a more expansive understanding of women's joy and wholeness. Lorde argues for the importance of the erotic as a source of power and deep feeling beyond "just sexual desire," expanding the meaning beyond the pornographic in order to counter the patriarchal oppression that shapes the lives of women. In fact, Lorde uses the word *satisfaction* and its variations about ten times in the short essay. In each instance, satisfaction is an outcome of accessing the power of the erotic. She writes, "The erotic is a measure between the beginning of our sense of self and the chaos of our strongest feelings. It is an internal sense of satisfaction to which, once we have experienced it, we know we can aspire."[12] For Lorde, the erotic is a vehicle for satisfaction, the process by which women become fully attuned to joy, completely inhabit their bodies, work, life experiences, spirituality, and community.[13]

Likewise, a number of contemporary scholars of Black feminism have taken up elements of Lorde's argument regarding the power of the erotic without adhering to the antipornography elements undergirding some aspects of "Uses of the Erotic." These scholars seek to read Black women's sexual pleasure and satisfaction against the grain of racial injury. Jennifer C. Nash places attention on ecstasy as opposed to injury within a "phallic economy."[14] Likewise, L. H. Stalling takes Lorde's erotic and "funks" it to produce "alternate orders of knowledge about the body and imagination that originate in a sensorium predating empires of knowledge."[15] Both Nash's and Stalling's work allow me to think dynamically about satisfaction as more than a reactionary reply to patriarchal violence. In particular, their work inclines me to think sex work as imaginative work that denies social stigma and reorders our understanding of Black women's pleasure and labor, which I do when analyzing Ann Petry's *The Street* (1946).[16]

Similarly, in her work on Black women's pleasure during the interwar years, Tara T. Green considers the multiplicity of pleasure in Black women's lives and their cultural production. She focuses on the restrictive role that respectability politics—the social mandate to behave in public with proper comportment in order to ensure the equal worth of African Americans in the eyes of the nation—has played in Black women's expression of pleasure. According to Green, pleasure is "for the self."[17] Her work, therefore, is invested in examining the ways Black women artists center their personal experiences of pleasure, with less emphasis placed on community or larger questions of justice.

Clearly, there are overlaps between the erotic, pleasure, and satisfaction as modes for considering the various ways Black women experience a sense of joy, fulfillment, contentment, and wholeness. I select the language of satisfaction (as opposed to that of pleasure or the erotic) in order to include in my analysis the kinds of joy and completion made possible through family, community, and political engagement—both within the works under scrutiny and for their writers. While I explore how Dorothy West imagined Black women's asexuality and queer family-making as a potential avenue to satisfaction, as well as Ann Petry's depiction of sex workers as viable models of Black women's community and heroism, I have purposefully elected not to focus exclusively on sexual pleasure in my formulation of Black women's satisfaction. Black feminist scholarship over the past forty years (some of which I cite) has done a remarkable job carving out space for considering the vexed and important role of sex and sexual autonomy for Black women. Enslavement and its long shadow have made Black women's sexual lives complex and more than worthy of scholarly attention. However, my interest in satisfaction stems from a desire to highlight other sites of pleasure (family, friends, work/labor, and leisure) that are no less complex or worthy of study in a mid-twentieth-century context. It is my desire to present a more expansive register along which Black women can experience satisfaction, which can include but is not limited to sex.

The literary works of Petry, West, Childress, and Brooks establish the fullness of experience, the joy of self-sufficiency, and a refusal to measure life by standards meant to exclude Black womanhood. There are, of course, erotic elements to these women's writings, but more than in sexual acts, I am interested in how these writers and their texts capture the idea of satisfaction as the deep feelings of self-worth and wholeness in the face of devaluation. I am also keenly aware of those moments when this sense of satisfaction compels characters to engage their communities. Thus, I'm tracking feelings and stances in relationship to the self and one's community that represent a sense of fullness and completion.

Toni Morrison beautifully theorizes a companion idea to satisfaction as I conceive of it in her essay "The Source of Self-Regard." In the piece, Morrison locates self-regard as nascent in Sethe's "Me? Me?" or—more fleshed out—in the freedom to choose your beloved, as in her novel *Jazz* (1992). She describes self-regard variously as "a reclamation of the self" or a placing value on oneself or in one's community and culture.[18] Overall, I think of satisfaction as an outcome of self-regard for Black women, much like the erotic as Lorde imagines it. This is to say, when a Black woman is able to access a deep sense of her own worth as a person, in opposition to prevailing national sentiment about her (particularly during the decades of segregation), then she is able to experience a sense of satisfaction. Satisfaction, then, is akin to what Kevin Quashie so eloquently describes in *Black Aliveness, or A Poetics of Being,* as Black aliveness: a turn to a Black world, "whose only cohering value is the rightness of black being, the possibility of black becoming."[19] I want to add satisfaction as a register of the Black world Quashie imagines, a world in which aliveness is registered through the personal because Black interiority is worth cultivating and living. The feeling of satisfaction can be fleeting and tenuous, but those flashes of self-regard and aliveness

Carrie Mae Weems, I Looked and Looked and Failed to See What So Terrified You *(Louisiana Project series), 2003. Digital print, 35¾ × 23¾ inches (each). Copyright Carrie Mae Weems. Courtesy of the artist and Jack Shainman Gallery, New York.*

facilitate the sense of completion that I search for in the texts under analysis.

Carrie Mae Weems's *I Looked and Looked and Failed to See What So Terrified You* from her 2003 Louisiana Project series is a profound visual representation of finding satisfaction in a world where the hegemonic (white and male) gaze finds Black women terrifying. The diptych photograph features the artist in a standing pose, holding a hand mirror up to her face. Weems (that is, the subject) makes no attempt to capture the gaze of the viewer because she beholds her own image (doubly). In this looking and looking again, Weems's subject erases the terror of the gaze and replaces it with her own validating form of looking. The viewer of *I Looked and Looked* remains outside of Weems's display of self-regard. Moreover, the viewer is not invited in to share the meaning they may be making with the woman in the mirror(s); she makes her own meaning. From the photograph's title, the external gaze is chastised for attempting to superimpose its feelings and meaning: the subject fails to see "what so terrified you" and, in so failing, is able to look lovingly and with satisfaction upon herself. The practice of self-regard on display in Weems's photograph sets the stage for how I think about mid-twentieth-century Black women's literary turns away from a white hegemonic viewer's gaze.

It is Weems's face turned inward that I want to model as reading practice but also that I see at work within the writers I study in this project. There are multiple possibilities for Black womanhood subjected to and protesting the creative, cultural, and political logics of nationalized white supremacy. Exploring writers like Petry, West, Childress, and Brooks, I approach from a variety of perspectives Black women's satisfaction amid Jim Crow and, in so doing, trace how each writer's vision revolves around a "monstrous turn."

I'm defining a *monstrous turn* as a turn away from the forms of life that are offered by the state and other hegemonic agents toward more radical forms of Black being. This time Toni Morrison's *Beloved* (1987) is a useful literary example that pushes characters to take monstrous turns. Sethe's murder/saving of Beloved from School Teacher and enslavement on Sweet Home plantation, that monstrous deed, turns the novel in profound ways into a rumination on the complexity of (re)memory, haunting, history, enslavement, and love among the formerly enslaved and their progeny. The hard choice that Sethe makes and has to live with weighs on her and becomes embodied in the form of Beloved. It is not until she is able to accept the act, and the care from the Black women who exorcise Beloved's ghost from her home (and heart), that she is able to utter those words of a nascent self-regard—"Me? Me?"—that I referenced earlier.

In turning toward the monstrous, I hope to provide a distinctive mode of reading Black freedom, personhood, gender and sexuality, and futurity within Black women's midcentury writing. Scholar Christina Sharpe names "monstrous" the brutality of the intimacies between the antebellum Black enslaved people and their white enslavers and the postbellum erasure of that brutality.[20] Yet, for my purposes I explore the works of the writers in this project for how they engage the United States' monstrous history of enslavement and postemancipation racial subjection by doing the monstrous work of revision. In fact, each writer covered in *Monstrous Work and Radical Satisfaction* returns in some way to the antebellum period in order to modify the narrative of Black women's roles under enslavement.

Petry, West, Childress, and Brooks engage the monstrous intimacies of slavery with an eye toward the various ways enslaved peoples' resistance might be read as damaging the brutality (to further evoke Sharpe's language) of the slave system and its postemancipation afterlife. For instance, Gwendolyn Brooks imagines her paternal grandfather's escape from enslavement in her autobiography *Report from Part One* (1972); Dorothy West's *The Living Is Easy* (1948) conjures as evidence of matrilineal integrity an enslaved ancestor who kills herself in the face of her enslaver's fickle brutality; Ann Petry writes a historical recasting of Tituba Indian's role in the infamous Salem witch trials; and both Petry and Alice Childress narrativize Harriet Tubman as an extraordinary heroine of Black resistance for young readers. While it would not be until Margaret Walker Alexander's 1966 novel *Jubilee,* the first neo-slave narrative, that modern African American novelists would turn to Black enslavement, Petry, West, Childress, and Brooks all imagined enslaved people as heroes and radical resistors in the 1940s and 1950s.[21] These women writers revise the dehumanization of enslavement by emphasizing how enslaved peoples always practiced the monstrous work of self-emancipation. Moreover, Petry, West, Childress, and Brooks turn to the antebellum to source Black radicalism as part and parcel of the experience of slavery. They offer us a portal into understanding the history of Black radicalism as longer and more narratively significant than traditional leftist narratives often allow.

So, while I revisit Black women's literature in such a way as to acknowledge the monstrous intimacies that shape Black and white life in the West (as Sharpe so eloquently outlines), like my authors, I do so without internalizing or centering those particular intimacies. Instead, I wonder if other intimacies are possible. How might these Black women's writings reappropriate the idea of the "monstrous" for those living during the Jim Crow era? I am particularly interested in the expansiveness and flexibility of the monstrous as a category to be deployed by Black cultural producers.

Indeed, the idea of Blackness and Black people as monstrous and monsters, respectively, has a long lineage in literary production, especially within the American literary context. In her crucial work *Playing in the Dark* (1992), Toni Morrison traces the American literary imagination's impulse to engage what she calls "the Africanist presence" as a vehicle for whiteness. Morrison observes that since its founding, the United States has wrestled with Blackness, enlisting the "resident [Black and enslaved] population" to play through "historical, moral, metaphysical, and social fears, problems, and dichotomies."[22] Morrison's study provides a clear and popularly accessible articulation of how canonical American literature made monsters out of Black characters to ensure the nation's investment in whiteness. Likewise, the gothic genre is deeply invested in the "racialization of monster and monstrosity."[23] As the American gothic is "haunted by slavery," the threat of Black subjection haunts gothic formulations of art.[24] Indeed, racial clichés remain intact well into the twenty-first century and undergird much of the discourse that surfaces around every senseless murder of a Black person in the name of supposed national safety and security.

But Black writers in the United States have been speaking a double and monstrous tongue for centuries. If the American imaginary has been so gothicized as to make Black people synonymous with monsters, Black American writers have also gothicized their American experience. Gothic discourse is a two-way street.[25] For instance, with the publication "On Being Brought from Africa to America" in her *Poems on Various Subjects, Religious and Moral* (1773), the poet Phillis Wheatley calls all to remember, though cast in "a diabolic die" by their European companions in the American colonies, "Negros, black as Cain," may, too, be "refin'd."[26] Wheatley's poetic turn rests in her unwillingness to subscribe to the sinister and inherent devaluation of Black and enslaved people as the biblical Cain figures of the Americas. As June Jordan remarks of Wheatley: "Following on her 'intrinsic ardor,' and attuned to the core of her own person, this girl, this first Black poet in America, had dared to refine herself from the house slave, to possibly, an angel of the Almighty."[27]

Additionally, if we zero in on the divine entitlements assumed by this early African in America, another thread emerges. Wheatley's evocation of Christian faith and diabolic Blackness is illuminated by an etymological tracing of the meaning of *monster*. For Renaissance-era readers, monsters were "signs sent by God, messages showing his will or his wrath."[28] Among seventeenth- and eighteenth-century readers, there was a sense that women's imagination could so reshape progeny (offspring and works of art) as to make it lack resemblance to expected forms. Monsters illustrate the generative potential of imagination and maternity. Wheatley's work, influenced by and paired with these Western meanings of monsters, surfaces the Black female imagination as a powerful episteme that counters and invents a different set of relations to the core values of the protonation. Early critical evaluation of the gothic genre finds the etymological connotations of *gothic* as signaling the "rude, wild, and irregular."[29] The negative nature of these early understandings remains embedded in any evocation of the gothic. For this reason, I augment other literary examinations of monsters and monstrosity, especially those that originate in the gothic genre, emerge out of horror fiction and film monster tropes, or find meaning by evoking psychoanalysis's "dark other."

The "Black monster" exists beyond imagined tropes. In order to extend previous avenues of analysis, I think it more generative for Black literary and cultural production to imagine monstrousness beyond an injurious mode of embodiment and to resist assuming the monstrous and monstrosity to be discursively pejorative.[30] How might we think of Black monstrosity as useful beyond delineating the racial limitations of the American imagination? If fear propagates the social and political othering of Black people from colonial to contemporary times, how have Black women writers offered different avenues for thinking beyond well-wrought narratives of monstrosity?

In "Mama's Baby, Papa's Maybe: An American Grammar Book," Hortense J. Spillers provides both phrasing and a theoretical foundation upon which I build to answer a number of my questions. In her canonical essay, Spillers illuminates the cultural "unmaking" of Black people by the African slave trade, as well as the "ungendering" of the enslaved person (the "captive") and their progeny (the "liberated") vis-à-vis Western conceptualizations of gender. Through the idea of ungendering, Spillers speculates that lack of access to Western gender roles leaves African Americans in vestibular relation to the versions of kinship and humanity that circulate in the United States. She arrives at this idea of ungendering through a material analysis of the hold of the ship and the arrangement of Black people in the hold: "the female in the 'Middle Passage,' as the apparently smaller physical mass, occupies 'less room' in a directly translatable money economy. But she is, nevertheless, quantifiable by the same rules of accounting as her male counterpart."[31] The reduction of Black people to financial objects stands at the center of captive Africans' (and their progeny's) lack of access to "patriarchilized" gendering and objectified dehumanization.[32] She explores what she terms the "hieroglyphics of the flesh," or the intergenerational transfer of symbolic and material injuries in the forms of hypercommodification and precarious dehumanization, to discuss the transfer of this ungendering from generation to generation.[33]

The duality of Spillers's notion of ungendering—the idea that it is produced out of the trauma of the Middle Passage and that it frees Black women from the burden of hegemonic gender expectations—is productive for my own thinking about monstrousness and satisfaction. Spillers's work within this duality is most clearly displayed as she ends "Mama's Baby, Papa's Maybe":

> This problematizing of gender places her [the Black woman], in my view, out of the traditional symbolics of female gender, and it is our task to make a place for this different social subject. In doing so, we are less interested in joining the ranks of gendered femaleness than gaining the *insurgent* ground as female social subject. Actually *claiming* the monstrosity (of a female with the potential to "name"), which her culture imposes in blindness, "Sapphire" might rewrite after all a radically different text for female empowerment.[34]

These concluding lines are orienting for *Monstrous Work and Radical Satisfaction*. Spillers encourages us to imagine new openings for a productive Black female monstrosity.

While Spillers returns to the hold of the ship to begin rethinking the role of gender and womanhood for enslaved people and their offspring, as well as signaling the insurgent potential of monstrosity, Sylvia Wynter turns to a critique of Enlightenment hierarchies to rethink the human.[35] Her attention to Sycorax in William Shakespeare's *The Tempest* (1623) is particularly interesting as I consider the role of the monstrous in Black women's writing.[36] Wynter draws attention to the play's (unsuccessful) attempts to erase the island's first inhabitant, Sycorax, Caliban's mother. Remembered as an absent presence in the play, Sycorax serves as a reminder that Black womanhood has long haunted Anglophone literature. Shakespeare's depiction of Caliban as a raced subject creates "a new category of the human, that of the subordinated 'irrational' and 'savage' *native* is now constituted as the lack of the 'rational' Prospero, and the now-capable-of-rationality Miranda, by the Otherness of his/its *physiognomic* 'monster' difference, a difference which now takes the *coding* role of sexual-anatomical difference."[37] Like Spillers, Wynter also references the monstrous, calling attention to Caliban's "'monster' difference." And, similar to Spillers, she is interested in rethinking the potential of such difference for reconfigurations of normative categories. For Wynter, that category is the Man-as-Human. Wynter's charge for Black studies is to encourage Black people's continued forging toward alternative humanity, one that allows itself to be haunted by figures like Sycorax.

Taken together, Spillers and Wynter frame my thinking and attending to alternative approaches to both womanhood and monstrosity. They force one to attend to those cultural productions that create roads to disruption rather than bridges to insertion if one intends to resist reinforcing hierarchies of race, gender, sexuality, and even humanity. For instance, if we return to the figure of Sycorax, she stands outside the construct of the Enlightenment's human, serving as a model of New World monstrosity that is denied by the West but worth reclaiming.

Thus, in exploring what I call the "monstrous work" and the "monstrous turn" in Black women's mid-twentieth-century literature, I offer readings of how these writers attempt to craft and claim narratives that seek to resist the traditional symbolics of being gendered woman in the United States. The alternative affective possibilities they make available to us in this current political moment far exceed those imagined by the state for African Americans, and they are monstrous to the state by virtue of their defiance. The monstrous turn, in particular, is best recognized as a shift away from those characterizations, formalistic narrative structures and imperatives, and interpersonal relationalities that are meant to imaginatively remedy Black exclusion.

In *Monstrous Work and Radical Satisfaction,* the monstrous work and the turn to this work take various forms. In chapter 1, it looks like centering sex workers, an enslaved "witch," and an escaped enslaved woman as potential and actual heroines in a non-Black world that marks them as criminals. In chapter 2, the turn looks like a woman who values and builds a matrilineal household in the face of domestic and national normative patriarchy. In chapter 3, the monstrous turn takes the form of amplifying the critical voice of a Black domestic worker as the moral and social center of U.S. political discourse. And, in the fourth chapter, the monstrous turn like reimagining the possible affiliations between Black people and animals. At the core of all these narratives, however, is a reconfiguring of the world with Black womanhood as the norm and the ethical center.

Radicalism in Black Women's Mid-Twentieth-Century Literature

From planned insurrections to fugitivity from enslavement, Black life has been infused with a desire for radical change. Black thinkers and activists have enacted a radical agenda since early enslavement. Angela Y. Davis observes in *Women, Culture, and Politics* (1989) that radicalism and radicals were rendered bogeymen within the post-Reagan era's anti-Sovietism: she reminds us that "radical simply means 'grasping things at the root.'"[38] Even earlier in the twentieth century, Marcus Garvey defines *radical* as a "label that is always applied to people who are endeavoring to get freedom."[39] Like Davis's critique of Reaganism, Garvey's definition of *radicalism* draws attention to the punitive nature of the term when the powerful apply it to delegitimize the "freedom dreams" of the less powerful. The simplicity of these definitions is inviting: collectively, they highlight the roots and goals of radicalism as freedom and the proactive ending of oppression as a source of collective empowerment. Thus, my aim in this project is to lean into Garvey's and Davis's open-ended definitions of *radicalism* to explore the literary freedom dreams of mid-century Black women writers—without completely losing sight of the term's relationship to leftist, anticapitalist politics.

In the decades after the Cold War's end, scholars like Brian Dolinar, Bill V. Mullen, Barbara Foley, Alan M. Wald, William J. Maxwell, James Edward Smethurst, Cheryl Higashida, and Mary Helen Washington, to name a few, provided literary and historical context to our understanding of the relationship between the Left and African American literary production from the Harlem Renaissance into the Cold War years.[40] Released in the shadow of the Cold War's end and sharing a 1999 publication date, Bill V. Mullen's *Popular Fronts,* James Edward Smethurst's *The New Red Negro,* and William J. Maxwell's *New Negro, Old Left* paint varied, valued, and vexed readings of Black literary artists, the orthodoxy of the Communist Party, and the radical Left. The payoff of Smethurst's work comes twofold: in its ability to reshape our periodization of the Harlem Renaissance (particularly its supposed end) and in its detailing of the Left's generic influence on the thematic and aesthetic shape of Black poetry during the 1930s and 1940s. Similarly, Mullen's book settles into Chicago to focus on the site as fostering the midwestern artistic renaissance of the 1930s and 1940s. In particular, Mullen captures a more reciprocal relationship between Black artists and the white members of the U.S. popular front and Communist Party. Mullen settles on what he refers to as the "Negro People's Front" to illuminate Black radicals' creative application of Communist policy and ideas to forge an "independent brand of radicalism," able to tend to the particular conditions of life in Chicago's Black Belt.[41] Maxwell's project is more aligned with a historical revision that seeks to rectify post-McCarthy critical amnesia around the influence of the Communist Party on African American literary and cultural production. These works signal increased interest in and freedom for scholars of Black cultural history to tell a nuanced story about the Black radical literary left at the end of the twentieth century, one unhindered by repressive Cold War politics in the United States.

While the role of Black women in the Left was formative, it is often not centered during discussions of mid-twentieth-century radicalism.[42] Claudia Jones was the Communist Party's most prominent Black woman organizer throughout the 1940s and 1950s. She stands as the most explicit example of the intersection between leftist and Black Feminist thought in the midcentury. Angela Davis mentions Jones among the five figures she profiles for her "Communist Women" chapter in *Women, Race, and Class* (1981).[43] And in *Left of Karl Marx* (2008), Carole Boyce Davies asserts that Jones's political perspective was "advanced well beyond the limitations of Marxism" because she was able to analyze workers' struggles through the

lenses of race and gender.[44] In her essay "An End to the Neglect of
the Problems of the Negro Woman!" published in *Political Affairs* in
June 1949, Jones argues for Black women's centrality to the workers'
struggle due to their combined status "as workers, as Negroes, and
as women."[45] She also highlights Black women's experiences as mass
organizers within their communities, arguing that they are an un-
tapped resource for leadership roles within the Communist Party.[46]
Much like her Black foremothers Maude White Katz and Louise
Thompson Patterson, who worked in the party during the 1930s,
Jones changed the party's agenda around Blackness and womanhood.[47] Women like Jones remind us that Black women have always
been present in the development of a more inclusive vision for the
traditional Left within the United States.

Centering Black women's leftist politics and prose resists the
anti-Communist occlusion of Black women as Marxists.[48] The impact and importance of Black women on the left in the United States
should be central to any history of midcentury African American
letters.[49] As Cheryl Higashida argues, "Women writers of the Black
Left worked within and against established forms to represent how
everyday lives of Black women, lesbians, and gay men were linked
with and transformative of internationalist projects."[50]

Although Jones and other Black women did work directly for the
Communist Party, there is space within the definition and study of
literary radicalism to include more intangible and less formal leftist and Communist Party work done by Black women. For instance,
in a 2000 interview, Sylvia Wynter, who worked for the Communist
Party internationally, reflected on how her growth as a thinker was
shaped by forces beyond Marxism.[51] And the more open-ended notions of radicalism articulated by Davis, which she articulated as a
member of the Communist Party USA, encourage consideration of
practices of radicalism that exceed traditional ideological and political modes. Petry, West, Childress, and Brooks all circulated among
Communist Party members or fellow travelers (or were themselves
fellow travelers), but each also imagines the radical work of Black
women, regardless of Communist Party affiliation or ideological
commitments, as work that is bound to the domestic and interpersonal lives of Black women.

Thus, *Monstrous Work and Radical Satisfaction* positions its scholarly interests at those literary sites among and between home spaces and workspaces. The texts under analysis focus on how one organizes a home, the alliances built and rebuilt around the Black family, friendships made between humans and nonhumans, and how to do one's work with dignity and purpose. The project thinks through the long-lingering failures of U.S. meritocracy and the continued success of social, political, and cultural Black exclusion by the state and other institutions predicated on white supremacy. I highlight modes of Black liberation in the midst of local, national, and international structures intent on confining and limiting Black (women's) lives and narratives.

Organization

The chapters that follow illuminate how Black women writers creatively projected space for self-ownership and self-articulation. Though unfolding in a sort of publication chronology, the chapters do not adhere strictly to a chronological or progressive narrative about race, gender, monstrosity, and literary studies. Instead, the sections each deal with some elemental turn away from the normative models offered to African American women on the cusp of national desegregation. The book's most profound investment is in exploring the new subject formations possible when we uncouple rights and respectability. What new worlds and new life work is made possible if we find joy in our ugly work, refuse marriage conventions as the only means for social connection, center the dignity of Black women's labor, or imagine the human to include animals and other life?

Like many of us, the writers I feature in this book wrote and worked on the cusp of promises of national inclusion. Like many Black women, these women produced a legacy despite the multiple jeopardies of race, gender, class, and sexuality. It is that legacy that is monstrous, serving as a beacon of how to create art and lives capable of weathering cultural shifts and political changes that rarely imagine Black women as capable but as always subject to gendered state violence. As Erica R. Edwards notes, many of the techniques central to the United States' long war on terror have been practiced on Black women since this country's origin: "Black women captives on the home front—on the plantation, on the chain gang, in the prison yard or solitary cell, in the car, in the front-yard garden, at the airport, on the sidewalk—served as test cases for the techniques of surveillance and torture that would be exported after 2001."[52] Therefore, each chapter of this project focuses on a single author, enabling me to pay careful attention to their depth and unique perspective on satisfaction as a resistance to captivity. And each chapter emphasizes various components of domestic work—for one's own family, for one's community, or for one's employers—to restore the importance of the home as a potentially radical site of national disruption.

Chapter 1 explores three works by Ann Petry—*The Street* (1946), *Harriet Tubman: Conductor on the Underground Railroad* (1955), and *Tituba of Salem Village* (1964)—focusing on what I call "ugly work." I argue that Petry's Black women protagonists engage in the radical refusal of both enslavement and the liberal integrationism of the midcentury by doing ugly work. From sex work to running away from enslavement to witchcraft, Petry illustrates that Black women's collective action and radical imaginations are dangerous to the status quo of the nation, from colonial to antebellum to modern times. She allows readers (adult and young adult) the space to imagine formulations of the monstrous and satisfaction that remap autonomy and freedom for midcentury Black women.

Chapter 2 shifts from the work that Black women do outside of the home to a consideration of how Black women reimagine the nuclear family and domestic sphere to their satisfaction. In this chapter, Dorothy West's 1930s editorial work is placed in conversation with her creative writing—specifically, *The Living Is Easy* (1948)—to develop the women-centered Black family as a potentially radical site for satisfaction. Although West published *The Living Is Easy* nearly twenty years before the *Moynihan Report* (1965), the novel grapples with national sentiments that flourished before and well after the infamous report's pathologizing of the Black family and women's roles within the domestic setting. I argue that West's fiction captures the possibilities of family formation as an alternative labor space for generating models of radical satisfaction.

In chapter 3, I turn directly toward traditional labor questions as they appear within the domestic setting by focusing on Alice Childress's Jim Crow–era domestic workers. Here I explore Childress's play *Florence* (1949) and her collection of short stories, *Like*

One of the Family: Conversations from a Domestic's Life (1956). I begin the chapter with Childress's FBI file, in order to consider how she writes from a position of what Simone Browne calls "dark sousveillance" or counterveillance, which is the tendency to observe authority in order to resist it.[53] Childress's work illustrates how American power structures saw the presumption of dignity among Black domestic workers as a threat. Overall, the chapter examines how domestic labor might be a source of Black women's satisfaction if they are treated with dignity as they work against racism and American nationalism.

Chapter 4 returns to the African American home space and family as a site of refusal. Unlike many feminist studies of domesticity, this final chapter proposes that we expose the Black subject's empowerment, citizenship, and right to life that come through nonreproductive avenues. This chapter brings together and considers the productive affiliations between Black people and nonhuman animals in Gwendolyn Brooks's *Maud Martha* (1953). I analyze dreams, desire, and hunger as tropes for challenging presumptive positivist beliefs around racial integration just as de jure racial segregation is on the verge of a societal shift. This chapter puts Brooks's work in conversation with contemporary race and animal studies and critiques of racial integration and its failure to take root in the late twentieth and early twenty-first centuries. I close *Monstrous Work and Radical Satisfaction* with the hopes, possibilities, and satisfaction that emerge from being illegible and politically at odds with the United States.

Through centering the literary and cultural texts produced by Ann Petry, Dorothy West, Alice Childress, and Gwendolyn Brooks during the Jim Crow era, *Monstrous Work and Radical Satisfaction* marks the potential of the monstrous as an aesthetic approach capable of placing Black women's satisfaction above the promises of national inclusion. The works of these Black women from an earlier era offer models of Black women's well-being in the face of national change and upheaval. *Monstrous Work and Radical Satisfaction* adds to the story of African American leftist work by centering Black women's writing on the domestic and labor experiences of Black women. These texts remain vital to readers, writers, and a nation still enmeshed in integration's failed logic.

CHAPTER 1

Ugly Work

Alterity and the "Ugly Work" of Black Life

In May 2020, the *New York Times* and PBS NewsHour named Ann Petry's 1946 novel *The Street* as the next pick for their social-media-based book club, Now Read This. The announcement followed closely on Houghton Mifflin's January 2020 reissue of Petry's debut novel, which holds the distinction of being the first novel written by an African American woman to sell over a million copies. Newly reissued, the novel features a refreshed cover with tasteful yellow and brown lettering alongside a feminine silhouette, which readers are no doubt meant to assume belongs to the novel's attractive protagonist, Lutie Johnson. The reissued text comes with an introduction by *New York Times* best-selling author Tayari Jones, who served as one of the discussion leaders for the book club.[1] The extensive contemporary cross-marketing of this novel is intriguing: Why reissue *this* book *now*? Why does this work continue to speak well into the twenty-first century?

At some level, an answer resides in the enduring questions raised in the first best-selling novel written by a Black woman. Focusing on Lutie Johnson's quest for sustaining work and financial security as she raises her young son in post–World War II Harlem, *The Street*'s durability rests in no small part on Petry's capacity to represent the multiple forms of oppression that African Americans continue to face. For instance, in the wake of the 2014 uprisings in Ferguson, Missouri, cultural critic Michael Eric Dyson urged a return to *The Street* in a *New York Times* opinion piece. Dyson lauded Petry's detailed examination of the dehumanization the police must enact in order to justify their senseless murder of a Black man.[2] In 2017, Tayari Jones urged a return to Petry's 1946 novel, again in the *New York Times*. She was moved to write about *The Street* amid the growing #MeToo

movement, arguing, "For Lutie there is no #MeToo movement.
Ronan Farrow will not be calling her for a quote. Her experience
more than fifty years ago is very similar to that of women today who
are poor and of color. She must save herself, understanding that there
will be devastating consequences for standing her ground."[3] Under
Jones's scrutiny, Petry's work stands as a mid-twentieth-century form
of Black literary resistance to the national silence around Black wom-
en's sexual assault and survival. Taken together, these two *New York
Times* pieces, written seventy years after the initial publication of *The
Street*, represent two distinct but intertwined sets of concerns available to contemporary readers thinking about the racialized and sexu-
alized violence afflicted upon the Black community under Jim Crow.

I would add that Petry's fiction resonates because the work is
able to take a variety of "monstrous turns" in the face of the racism,
sexism, and labor exploitation that led Jones and Dyson to call for a
return to her work in the early twenty-first century. As I stipulate in
this book's introduction, monstrous turns are those literary maneu-
vers Black women writers make in order to imagine and aestheticize
possibilities against the forms of gender, racial, sexual, and class oppression experienced by Black people in the United States. These
turns require moves away from constructions of the American Black
subject as incorporated citizen. In particular, Petry's *The Street* emphasizes the impact of racial and sexual violence on Black women
when they are primary caregivers and breadwinners, victims of racist
hiring and social practices, and potential victims of sexual assault. As
the novel's protagonist ends the text as a fugitive for murder, normative citizenship is foreclosed to her.

Additionally, when one turns to Petry's young adult writing, placing it in conversation with her best-selling novel *The Street*, a richer picture of Black life emerges: fugitivity, alterity, and forms of liberation
that exist outside normative inclusion. In this chapter, I assemble three
of Petry's novels focused on people of African descent: *The Street* and
her two young adult (YA) historical fiction novels, *Harriet Tubman:
Conductor on the Underground Railroad* (1955) and *Tituba of Salem Village* (1964).[4] From *The Street* to her young adult novels, we see Black
women create dynamic life options from limited opportunities. Petry's
Black women characters chart new histories and futures in the face of
power and whiteness in the United States.[5]

Whether enslaved or "free," Petry's Black women characters are perpetual others to the nation. All three novels build narrative capacity for characters whose alterity marks them as socially, politically, and economically excluded from the full benefits of U.S. citizenship. This is particularly true in her two young adult novels, which feature enslaved women who were never historically meant to experience citizenship. Anticipating the late twentieth-century turn to the neoslave narrative in Black literature, Petry returns to Harriet Tubman and Tituba Indian to claim them as models of Black women's capacity to self-liberate in the face of systemic threats and violence. These historical figures also tie Petry to the leftist tradition of educating Black young people in nontraditional heroes for race pride and uplift.

In order to get at Petry's models of self-liberation, I read the alterity among Petry's Black women characters through the lens of "ugliness." The word *ugly* comes from the Old Norse *uggligr*, meaning "to be dreaded."[6] Petry's texts encourage us to think about the productivity of leaning into ugliness or the dread Black women generate in the American imaginary in order to imagine new possibilities. I follow the common understanding of ugliness as suggesting a quality or characteristic that sits in opposition to normative beauty and beauty culture. Working both Petry's exploration of beauty's foil, as well as the ways fear and dread become associated with Black women, each text offers a version of Black possibility that comes from a character's embrace of their ability to generate perceived dread in others.

More particularly, an embrace of ugliness in the form of cultural dread functions as a prerequisite for what I call "ugly work." Ugly work is the work that Petry's Black women characters carry out; it stands in opposition to the "respectable," "legitimate," socially condoned forms of labor expected of Black women. Ugly work is work that is done for one's own benefit or to benefit the lives of other Black and oppressed people. I enter these texts to explore what Petry imagines for the possibilities of Black women who embrace alterity and the "ugly work" of Black life.

The Best-Selling Outsider

Black alterity was more than a fictional motif for Ann Petry. In an autobiographical sketch published in 1988, when she would have

been nearing eighty years old, Petry reflects on her career's resilience. She determines that her continued production and ambition
as a writer are due in no small part to her outsider status. In this way,
she fashions herself similar to another Black New Englander, W. E. B.
Du Bois, who spoke of his time at New England's (and America's)
most prominent educational institution as such: "I was in Harvard,
but not of it."[7] Similarly, Petry recounts New England as a "hostile
environment for a black family," though hers had been rooted in
Connecticut for four generations.[8] She begins and ends this autobiographical sketch by calling herself an "outsider, a maverick," "not
a member of the club," pointing out the oxymoronic status of being a
Black New Englander.[9] Although she was a New Englander by birth
and upbringing, Petry, like most African Americans in the North-
east, expresses an understanding of the long-lingering affective and
de facto shadow of both slavery and racial segregation in the Northern regions of the nation.

When she reflected on her literary influences, Petry named
Harriet E. Wilson as an ancestor. Both women hailed from New
England and wrote with Black audiences in mind.[10] Likewise, both
were committed to exposing anti-Black racism as sowed in the soil of
the entire nation, region notwithstanding. She writes: "Having been
born black and female, I regard myself as a survivor and a gambler,
writing in a tradition that dates back to 1859 when *Our Nig*, the first
novel written by a black woman in this country, was published in
Boston, Massachusetts."[11] Wilson's semi-autobiographical novel's full
title is expository: *Our Nig; or, Sketches from the Life of a Free Black, in
a Two-Story White House, North; Showing That Slavery's Shadows Fall
Even There*. Though not an enslaved person, Wilson reveals "slavery"
as merely one iteration of the American ethos of white supremacy
that shaped the nation, regardless of geography, during the antebellum period and beyond.

Petry's naming of her own literary legacy is important for a number of reasons. First, it runs counter to much of the scholarship on the
author, which has focused on *The Street*, often with the stated assumption that the text belongs exclusively to the American naturalist/
realist tradition of protest fiction. Moreover, the novel's scholarship historically framed the writer and *The Street* as a derivative of
Richard Wright's *Native Son* (1940). An early scholar of the African

American novel tradition, Robert A. Bone, lumps *The Street* in with a set of lesser texts, which he describes as "Wright School novels."[12] Although he labels Petry's novel an "eloquent successor to *Native Son*," Bone finds the book wanting for the in-depth social analysis one expects from protest fiction.[13] Likewise, Bernard W. Bell's crucial early taxonomy of novelists writing before the 1950s centers Richard Wright. Bell is less critical of Petry's novel than Bone, opening up some generative space outside of Wright's shadow for considering her intervention, which, he argues, is the "demythologizing of American culture and Afro-American character."[14] Relatedly, Mary Helen Washington attributes the shortfalls of *The Street* to Wright's naturalistic influence. She suggests that rigid adherence to the period's generic conventions harms womanhood: "The form of social protest is so inimical to women that they are often depicted in this fiction as victimizers."[15] Even in asserting that *The Street* is a novel "unlike any other in American literary history," Farah Jasmine Griffin indirectly invites comparisons regarding the lineage and significance.[16] Under the scrutiny of these venerable scholars, a particular version of Petry's acclaimed novel's shortfalls and merits continues to have resonance. Petry's naming of her influence offers an alternative way to trace her importance to African American literary canon formation, which is often still seen through the lens of historical and literary adjacency to a somewhat limiting aesthetic and to Richard Wright's enduring (but stifling) genius. Her naming her own literary pedigree undermines Wright's claim on her career.

Second, tapping into the Black New England tradition allows Petry to narrate the violent nature of white Northerners when they encounter Black people and thereby show that the reach of Jim Crow segregation and violence extends well beyond the American South.[17] For example, in a short story entitled "Witness," Petry casts the shadow of Southern justice in upstate New York, calling on the tropes of endangered white womanhood, patriarchal violence, and the lynch mob. "Witness" follows Charles Woodruff, a Black man who has taken a job teaching high school English in a small New York town. Woodruff, leaving work late one evening, notices seven white teenage students who appear to be kidnapping a white girl named Nellie. After he attempts to intervene, the boys rough up and take Woodruff hostage as well. He becomes the story's titular

witness to Nellie's assault. With his back turned away from the assault but within earshot, Woodruff listens to the violence and is
forced to "touch" Nellie after the boys finish assaulting her. Woodruff
realizes the conundrum into which the teenagers have placed him:
if he reports the crime, the boys will accuse him of raping Nellie,
and the girl, having been hooded during the assault, will not argue
otherwise. Woodruff considers his options, thinking, "Would the
police believe him? The school board? The PTA? 'Where there's
smoke there must be fire.' 'I'm not going to let my daughter stay in
his class.' "[18]

Ultimately, Woodruff opts to leave town, a reverse migration, because he knows the limits of white liberalism. In the space of this
short story, Petry reveals her mastery of character, perspective, sus-
pense, and racial horror and also demonstrates a capacity to tap into
the dual social realities that inform much of her work: first, anti-
Black violence is not geographically limited to the American South,
and second, sexual violence is often used as a tool of terror by the
white patriarchy. The political stakes and the expert technical execu-
tion on display in "Witness" and in many of the other short stories
in the *Miss Muriel* collection challenge the traditional literary scholarship that pigeonholes Petry's work as derivative of Wright's early
penchant for racial protest.

Even before her seventh decade, Petry had a capacious sense of the
novel's function in American society. In "The Novel as Social Criticism," an essay published in 1950, she argues for an expanded understanding of the social-critique novel, proposing that such novels are
informed not only by Marxism but also by the Bible, Greek tragedies,
and Shakespeare.[19] Taking a transhistorical approach to both Anglo
and American literatures, Petry argues neither for nor against the
validity of texts pressed into protest/proletariat/naturalist genres by
critics. Rather, she highlights the long tradition in which artists har-
ness the capacity of literature to open possibilities for social change.
If one understands Petry's relationship to the work of literature as pri-
oritizing social change for the urban Black working poor, then questions of genre become less significant.

Ultimately, my aim here is not to deny Wright's influence on Petry
but rather to provide a richer landscape for understanding the fiction
Petry writes after *The Street*. Her young adult novels and her short

fiction are part of her radical representational and pedagogical work, even as they do not fall into the category of "social protest" fiction.[20] They point to her wide understanding of the social change that is possible through literary production. Moreover, her commitment to being and writing from the perspective of an outsider invites us to think dynamically about the monstrous turn toward ugly work that Petry makes in order to center self-liberation and satisfaction among Black women characters.

Ugliness as Radical Resistance

Ugliness and beauty, like race and gender, are socially constructed and culturally specific.[21] And both are, in fact, tied to race: normative beauty standards have historically been used to marginalize and exclude Black women from accessing capital and power. As Tressie McMillan Cottom argues, "Beauty isn't actually what you look like; beauty is the preferences that reproduce the existing social order," and it is meant to "exclude blackness."[22] And even when Black people develop counternarratives about beauty, they are being inclusive in a way that is "contingent upon capitalism."[23] What I take from her thinking about beauty is how it is best understood as a commodity that one may conditionally hold but that always necessitates the exclusion (or presumed ugliness) of an Other—namely, Blackness. Rejecting this commodity and its intent to affirm that status quo, Cottom makes an argument for ugliness not as a form of self-loathing but as a mode of political critique for Black womanhood. She argues for Black women's embrace of ugliness not as some sort of internalized self-hatred but as a means of naming what the United States has done to Black women in the name of beauty. Cottom is refusing to internalize a model of beauty that is meant to demean and exclude her as a Black woman; instead, she is drawing attention to the reproduction of social and cultural inequities that shape Black women's lived experiences in the United States. I believe Ann Petry arrives at a similar space of thinking in the mid-twentieth century. Taken together, Petry's and Cottom's works speak to the longevity of the beauty conundrum for Black women.

From the 1940s to the early 1960s, there is a thread of ugliness and its possibility in Petry's work. Moreover, I would argue that Petry is working toward a version of ugliness that approaches the conundrum of Black worth and beauty in a way that is different from the catch-phrase that was popularized during the Black Power movement of the late 1960s and early 1970s: *Black is beautiful.* Instead of merely offer-ing up a version of Black beauty to counter the Eurocentric aesthetics that render Blackness other than beautiful, Petry allows ugliness to model a way out of normative modes of inclusion. It is not that she's uninterested in race pride, per se, but that her investment resides in exploring the possibilities of Black life outside the confines of beauty discourse.

While many people will recall the beauty of *The Street*'s Lutie Johnson, Petry also incorporates characters, Mrs. Hedges and Min, who are never described as beautiful or attractive. What is distinc-tive about both Mrs. Hedges and Min is that they carve out a space for themselves in the world once they center their self-regard and refuse to be limited by beauty standards that are not available to them as Black working women. Mrs. Hedges does her "ugly work" of refusal through the underground economy (prostitution) and Min through participating in Black folk traditions (root work). Each woman's choice to bypass (supposedly) legitimate means of achiev-ing their personal goals signals the novel's investment in portraying how the marginalized create ways for themselves outside the nor-mative. Petry's mobilization of ugliness, then, seems also to align with Theodor W. Adorno's characterization of ugliness as inherently oppositional to standards of form and normativity.[24] In this way, my approach with her texts also considers Black workingwomen's lives and their physical bodies while refusing to align them with failure, inadequacy, or tragedy. As Lori Merish notes, the narratives workingwomen wrote often fight against "the tragic mode," which "conscripted them into" naturalism's "plot of decline."[25] While Petry was not herself a workingwoman—she was decidedly middle class and professionally trained as a pharmacist—she does offer an al-ternative to failure or decline to many of her working-class women characters who manage to carve out spaces of relief for themselves from systems meant to demean and disregard them.

Though I want to emphasize Petry's mobilization of ugliness, I also want to note that she often foils ugliness and beauty in *The Street*. For instance, *The Street* traffics in traditional beauty standards, but only to illustrate how the spoils of beauty remain elusive to African American women. One should be reminded of Cottom's critique, which takes beauty to be so associated with whiteness that those who are Black are only able to access beauty via proximity to whiteness.[26] So although Lutie is perceived to be beautiful, her Blackness corrupts whatever spoils she might gain from it. Thus, Lutie's beauty is a burden. But it is also a resource: a means by which a Black working-class woman can lift herself out of racialized poverty. With this in mind, many critics have taken up the concern of Lutie Johnson's beauty and her value in the novel's sexual marketplace.[27]

Critical attention to Lutie's proximity to prostitution and her resistance to such work often assumes her investment in bourgeois respectability politics and her faith in the American Dream promised by the coupling of liberal democracy and capitalism. Interestingly, Lawrence P. Jackson sources Lutie's near-Victorian virtue to Petry's own "clubwoman" sexual politics and her desire to capture the Black middle class and the white liberals as her reading audience.[28] Though the novel begins with Lutie searching for an apartment in Harlem, flashbacks reveal that Lutie arrives at 116th Street having freshly left her failed marriage. Her marriage's failure can be sourced to the two years she spends separated from her husband and son as a live-in domestic worker for the Chandlers, a white family living in Connecticut. Lutie's proximity to the Chandlers increases her awareness of financial security promised by adherence to the ideals of American capitalism in detrimental ways. Mr. and Mrs. Chandler expose Lutie to their rules for upward mobility with no mention of the inequality inherent in the system of which they are part and beneficiaries:

> When she brought the coffee into the living room, after dinner, the conversation was always the same.
> "Richest damn country in the world——."
> "Always be new markets. If not here in South America, Africa, India——Everywhere and anywhere——."
> "Outsmart the next guy. Think of something before anyone else does. Retire at forty——."[29]

The text notes that Lutie has "absorbed some of the same spirit. The belief that anybody could be rich if he wanted to and worked hard

enough and figured it out carefully enough" (43). Enamored with
the Chandlers' home and lifestyle, Lutie places her faith in the
American Dream's meritocracy. Keith Clark reads Lutie as the "anti-
heroine" of *The Street* due to her "naivete" regarding the mythos of
the American Dream.[30] But arguably, Lutie is not naive; in my view,
she genuinely desires her portion with an American type of greed
that is voraciously global in its reach. We realize this when she
watches, along with the Chandler family, as Mr. Chandler's brother
kills himself on Christmas morning. The narrator notes that Lutie
"didn't lose her belief in the desirability of having money, though she
saw the mere possession of it wouldn't necessarily guarantee happiness" (49). Lutie seems committed to American capitalism even as
she remains critical of it.[31] As Candice M. Jenkins would say, Lutie
is motived by the salvific wish, which Jenkins defines as "a longing
to protect or save black women, and black communities more generally, from narratives of sexual and familial pathology, through the
embrace of conventional bourgeois propriety in the arenas of sexuality and domesticity."[32] Lutie refuses the ugly work of prostitution in
favor of salvific longing.

In spite of, or perhaps because of, Lutie's commitment to capitalist
ideals, the novel unfolds as an illustration of how Lutie's inability to
access the American Dream is a result of racism and sexism. Working
for the Chandlers, Lutie's experiences are shaped by "Jane Crow."[33]
Particularly acute are those stereotypes about Black women's sexual
availability and lasciviousness. For instance, Mrs. Chandler and her
friends admire Lutie's looks but seek to diminish her through sexu-
alizing her: "Whenever she entered a room where they were, they
stared at her with a queer, speculative look. Sometimes she caught
snatches of their conversation about her. 'Sure she's a wonderful
cook. But I wouldn't have any good-looking colored wench in my
house. Not with John. You know they're always making passes at
men. Especially white men'" (40–41). This logic is a holdover from
the nineteenth-century model of true womanhood, which, Hazel V.
Carby notes, demanded that white women "repress all overt sexuality" while Black women were, in contrast, depicted as overtly sexual.[34]
These women are rehearsing long and tired tropes of racialized, patriarchal white supremacy. Lutie is acutely aware that their deni-

gration of her propriety maintains their myths of white male sexual innocence and white women's sexual purity at her expense (41). I want to highlight, then, that Lutie is not lacking in race or gender consciousness, even as she continues to be motivated by the possibility of upward mobility. However, she desires that mobility through nonsexual means. Her growing political consciousness sits uneasily alongside her desire to access the American Dream; this is one of the most important tensions in her characterization.

One of the novel's central concerns, then, is how Western conceptions of beauty work against Black women. In addition to placing the exchange between Mrs. Chandler and her friends into a historically racist and sexist context, the narrative does the secondary work of offering various revelations regarding the dangerous limitations of Western notions of beauty when applied to Black women. In this way, one cannot separate the fatal reality of capitalism for Black womanhood in a culture where one's access to power and capital are aligned with beauty for women. Lutie, though attractive, can never amass enough beauty to get her access to hegemonic (white male) power and capital. Again, Cottom is useful here: "Beauty is for white women, if not for all white women. If beauty is to matter at all for capital, it can never be for black women."[35] In their consensus, these Connecticut white women affirm the universality of Lutie's beauty. Lutie is even the same shape as the wealthy and white Mrs. Chandler: she fits "perfectly" into the cast-off clothing that Mrs. Chandler attempts to give her (50). So her proximity to white standards of beauty would seem to mark her potential for upward mobility, at least within the Black public sphere. But, as the novel illustrates, beauty constructs that center whiteness tend not to materialize in productive ways for working-class Black women like Lutie.

Petry offers a critique of beauty and normativity as foundational to Black progress. Beyond her time with the Chandlers, there is a case to be made that nearly every encounter Lutie has in Harlem finds her arousing desire in those who see her. Boots Smith, the Harlem nightclub musician who promises her a place in his band as a singer, reneges because his boss, Mr. Junto, has marked Lutie for his own fantasy of sexual conquest. And William Jones, the superintendent of the 116th Street apartment building into which Lutie and her son Bub move after her marriage to Jim dissolves, also wants her. All of these examples of Black men's desire for Lutie point to the larger problem of beauty that Petry is putting forth: it fails Black women.

One of the most telling examples of this failure in the novel comes in the form of the building superintendent, Jones. Worming his way into Bub's life while Lutie is away at work, Jones uses the relationship with her son to be close to objects that are close to Lutie's body: "He picked [the can of talcum] up and looked at it. She sprinkled this under her arms and between her legs—that's how she would smell when he got close to her. Just like this. He opened the top of the can and sprinkled some of the powder in his hand" (107–8). Ultimately, Jones attempts to drag Lutie to the basement and rape her, only to be interrupted by Mrs. Hedges. But even Mrs. Hedges, whose complex role I will soon explore more fully, admires Lutie's beauty, telling Jones that he'd better stay away from Lutie because Mr. Junto intends to make use of her desirability for himself—in this case as a prostitute for his whites-only brothel in the Sugar Hill section of Harlem (238). All of this desire, compelled by her universally recognized beauty, proves to negatively affect Lutie's capacity to secure the American Dream she wishes for her and Bub. As Trudier Harris observes, "Lutie's struggle is constant, for the men who control money offer it to her only at the price of her body."[36] Her beauty and presumed sexual availability conspire to assist in the tragic end of her family. Though a potential resource, beauty has very little lasting value for Lutie and, in fact, places her in harm's way. The white women and the Black men who sexualize Lutie treat her as the commodity that beauty often entails for women, attempting to rob her of the agency she most desires: legitimate, upward mobility via the American Dream.

Perhaps instead of beauty, ugliness might be mobilized against white supremacy. Petry models what Yetta Howard describes as "a way to encounter modes of being and representing that exist outside normative paradigms of sexuality and textual practice."[37] Moving away from Lutie as both the protagonist and the embodiment of feminine beauty, let us turn toward Mrs. Hedges, who provides the counterexperience of beauty within the novel. A focus on Mrs. Hedges is meant not to deny the racism and sexism that conspire to undermine a character like Lutie but to consider how Petry uses

Mrs. Hedges to offer a way of moving within the systemic inequities of race and gender.

A sublime figure, Mrs. Hedges offers an alternative way for a Black woman to organize her relationship to her body and to exist within a capitalist framework—the framework within which Lutie wishes in vain to purchase the particular form of subjectivity that is promised by capitalism. Not long after meeting Lutie Johnson, readers meet Mrs. Hedges through Lutie's perspective. Upon first entering the apartment on 116th Street in Harlem, Lutie's eyes take in what she describes as "an enormous bulk of a woman," "very black," with a "rich" and "pleasant" voice, and with eyes as "still and as malignant as the eyes of a snake" (8–9). Mrs. Hedges represents more than Lutie can take in, and being "enormous," she represents the possibility of existence outside the notions of beauty that hold Lutie hostage. Examples abound within the novel of Lutie's awe and disgust when she looks upon Mrs. Hedges. Situating Mrs. Hedges's characterization through Lutie's perspective entwines the two characters in ways that work to highlight the relationship between beauty and ugliness that are important to the novel's critique of the former. Where Lutie is the same shape and size as the white Mrs. Chandler, Mrs. Hedges is corporeal excess. Where Lutie seeks legitimate work, Mrs. Hedges chooses a life of vice in which she is in a parasitic relationship to other women's sexuality. Her size, her line of work, her ease with living on the street conspire to move her away from the model of respectability and normativity that serve as a specter of possibility for Black women seeking a piece of the American Dream.

When readers accept Mrs. Hedges through Lutie's mediated perspective, she appears as a nosy neighbor. But Petry uses shifts in perspective to offer us a lens outside of Lutie's view. The young mother is correct to mistrust Mrs. Hedges's intentions for her. Her interest in Lutie is rooted in her sense of Lutie's value on the racialized sexual marketplace. As the proprietor of a brothel run out of her first-floor apartment, Mrs. Hedges spends her days sitting in her apartment window on the lookout for potential sex workers and clients. Several scholars have spent time interrogating Mrs. Hedges's function in *The Street*. For instance, an early reclamation comes in Marjorie Pryse's consideration of Mrs. Hedges as a "deist," an influential figure on 116th Street with little desire to disrupt the story's naturalistic outcome.[38]

However, Evie Shockley describes Mrs. Hedges as a gothic figure, made inhuman and hauntingly symbolic of Lutie's fate.[39] Finally, Carol E. Henderson's reading of Mrs. Hedges zeroes in on the character's body, scarred as a result of narrowly escaping a basement fire as an unhoused newcomer to New York City. Mrs. Hedges's scars, in turn, allow her to escape the racial and gender dynamics that entrap Lutie. Henderson observes that Mrs. Hedges "presents the most compelling example of bodily scarring that is directly attributable to class mobility and economic gain."[40]

Although Mrs. Hedges does have some genuine financial stability and peace of mind, it is her capacity to revise her relationship to beauty and desirability, to lean into the "revulsion" that her body elicits from other people, that she mobilizes in her own favor (241). But I would not necessarily limit this gain, as Henderson does, to her scarring. Petry notes that even before she was visibly scarred, many related to Mrs. Hedges's body as though it were a "monstrosity" (241). Again, this has most to do with her "unfeminine" size and darker skin color. She stands in starkest contrast to Lutie's "feminine" physique and medium-brown skin tone, both of which mark Lutie as more proximate to whiteness, more suitable for employment within both Black and white spaces.

Readers are able to consider colorism and "pretty privilege" in a moment when the narrative perspective shifts from Lutie's to Mrs. Hedges's. The transition both reveals the backstory leading to the latter's scarring and details how the scars opened up the possibility for her relative stability. Lindon Barrett characterizes Petry's chronological jumps and shifts in character perspective as staging a compression of narrative time and space.[41] This compression has the effect of allowing readers to begin to understand Mrs. Hedges (as well as other characters in the novel) as complex and haunted by a past that far exceeds what Lutie can access. After Mrs. Hedges saved Lutie from the rape, the two women find themselves at Mrs. Hedges's kitchen table, and her proximity to Lutie's feminine beauty causes Mrs. Hedges to consider her own lack of beauty. In a flashback, Mrs. Hedges recalls her social ostracization in her hometown in Georgia, homelessness upon moving to Harlem, and, finally, the basement fire that she escaped by crawling through "a narrow aperture not really big enough for the bulk of her body" (244). Escaping death but scarred by the fire, Mrs. Hedges refuses romantic overtures from Junto in favor of a relationship that is best characterized as a business partnership. In claiming a sort of professional life as opposed to following her own romance plot, Mrs. Hedges models autonomy outside of normative coupling conventions and forms of labor legitimized by the state. Her ugliness as a physical attribute yields productive considerations regarding how the ugly work of prostitution might free her from the gender and racial stereotypes that have limited her prospects throughout her life.

Mrs. Hedges's story is not unlike that of many Black people from the American South that would migrate to New York City and other urban contexts as part of the Great Migration's first and second waves. Mrs. Hedges moves from the American South (Georgia) to the North (New York) in an attempt to renegotiate the terms of her life in the world. In the words of Saidiya Hartman, she is in the cohort of Black women "rushing to the city to escape the plantation and intent on creating a new life in the context of a new enclosure."[42] Often attracted to urban centers for their promises of professional opportunity and freedom from the large- and small-scale violence of Southern segregation, women like Mrs. Hedges would have found the Northern labor market shaped by the same sort of bigotry, racism, and sexism they had sought to escape.

Many Black working women supplemented, or altogether replaced, their formal wage work with underground work. In *Sex Workers, Psychics, and Numbers Runners,* historian LaShawn Harris traces New York City's underground economy of Black working women during the first decades of the twentieth century. These working women took on a diverse set of jobs that paid off-the-books or were adjacent to the formal and legal labor markets. According to Harris, their "refusal to permit structural constraints and detractors from shaping their labor and personal decisions" marks their impact on labor history.[43] Petry, working from 1941 to 1944 as a journalist for the left-leaning weekly the *People's Voice,* developed a knack for reportage, allowing her to deploy literary realism as a mode for treating the complex living arrangements of Harlem's Black working-class inhabitants, particularly its women. While Mrs. Hedges does not take on legitimate work in addition to her criminal occupation, she was historically part of the domestic and working-class community before suffering the physical and psychological ailments that accompany her burns.

I do not in any way want to glamorize Mrs. Hedges's personal trauma or her role within a marketplace of Black women's objectification and sexual exploitation as a proprietor of a brothel. Because Mrs. Hedges is in business with Junto, the enigmatic and powerful white man who runs Harlem nightclubs and a brothel in Sugar Hill that caters exclusively to white men, she remains bound to the racist and sexist exploitation of Black women by the white establishment. In fact, applying a Marxist lens to *The Street,* Bill V. Mullen argues that Lutie ends the novel "the fetishized object of two slave markets, both Junto's and Hedges."[44] So, while Lutie is developing a political consciousness throughout the novel, she is unable to fully materialize an exit from her oppression due to gender and race objectification—something for which Mrs. Hedges is partially responsible.

However, Petry presents a more complex narrative of black-market relations and asks readers to consider the forms of sociality created by the sex marketplace in Harlem. In this context, Mrs. Hedges is both part of and in excess of the midcentury exploitative systems in which all the Black women of Harlem are embedded. If one assumes that the easy delineation between exploiter and exploited within the context of the Black community can be maintained, then Lutie is a victim and Mrs. Hedges is nothing more than part of the larger scheme meant to victimize Black women of the street. But such thinking disallows the possibilities, however limited, that Mrs. Hedges makes for herself and the other young Black women that come into her orbit. Mrs. Hedges introduces to the text what Cathy J. Cohen might describe as "a politics of deviance."[45] She and the women who work for her carve out lives for themselves within the informal economy of sex work. Lutie refuses to imagine their lives as anything but sordid.

Yet, I believe Mrs. Hedges and the women who work out of her apartment are what Saidiya Hartman describes as "wayward": "The wayward were guilty of a manner of living and existing deemed dangerous, and were a risk to the public good."[46] Extending Hartman's configuration of the aesthetics of beauty when describing Black living under and after Jim Crow, I want to consider the ugly experiments of Black life, as well. While I believe Black life can be and often is beautiful, I want to make room for Black artists who maintain an aesthetic outside the confines of the hegemonic discursive push for beauty.[47] I consider Black waywardness without gesturing toward an elevation of beauty.

Petry's depiction of Mrs. Hedges' apartment becomes a commentary on the underground economics, a deviant and wayward space that offers a counter to domestic labor exploitation by the white employers of many working-class Black women in the 1930s and 1940s. Of course, prostitution can be sexual exploitation. But Petry does not linger over that element of the work and the working relationships between Mrs. Hedges and the women of her brothel. Instead, Mrs. Hedges's apartment provides a form of community that Lutie fails to utilize because she idealizes Black middle-class propriety and morality. Contrast Lutie's decision with that of the minor character Mary, who lives with and works for Mrs. Hedges. Recovering from her burns after leaving the hospital, Mrs. Hedges initially takes Mary into her home to assist her with cooking, cleaning, and running errands. The two women are described as drawn to each other out of mutual need. Just as Mrs. Hedges needs support due to her medical condition, Mary is "dejected" when she first arrives to live with Mrs. Hedges. But the narrator describes Mary as having "blossomed out" under the older woman's care (248). This notion that Mrs. Hedges grows and cultivates Mary is a powerful metaphor for how we might think of Petry's representation of sex work in that it suggests that such labor might produce natural and generative growth.

Mrs. Hedges's philosophy on both sex workers and johns seems to come close to Cynthia M. Blair's argument in *I've Got to Make My Livin'*: Black sex workers "redefined the relationship of prostitution to black urban leisure to black community areas."[48] Beyond mixing the residential and commercial status of her apartment, Mrs. Hedges understands that she and the women she employs are selling escape and leisure among Harlem's working-class men. Once she realizes there is a market for young women like Mary among Black men in Harlem looking for "a means of escape in exchange for a few dollar bills," Mrs. Hedges's apartment functions at some level as a social way station. Mrs. Hedges takes in "lonesome, sad-looking girls just up from the South, or little girls who were tired of going to high school, and who had seen too many movies and didn't have the money to buy all the things they wanted," or young women "who had been married and woke up one morning to discover their husbands had moved out" (252). In all these versions of wayward women brought to sex work, the common denominator is that they no longer subscribe to the trappings of legal avenues of work toward upward mobility and social legitimacy. The novel does not use the language of coercion when describing how the women come to Mrs. Hedges's apartment. Mrs. Hedges and her employees thrive within her system, which sits alongside the legitimate economic system within which Lutie seeks employment and progress. What distinguishes these young women from Lutie is their lack of commitment to the sort of bourgeois propriety that ultimately robs Lutie of her son and compels her to embrace a fugitive lifestyle by the novel's end.

It is relatively easy to pathologize Mrs. Hedges for her scars or moralize her role as a madam. Still, Petry is clear that Mrs. Hedges provides the sort of safety and community that many young women would not have in the traditional labor market or traditional relationships. Although it is not a utopia—poverty, unhappiness with the grind of sex work, etc. prevail in Mrs. Hedges's brothel—it is a space away from the white gaze and the unjust labor conditions of the more legitimized domestic labor market. Again, when Mary falls in love with a young sailor who has no money left to pay for sex with her, Mrs. Hedges goes against her better business judgment and allows the two to spend the night together on credit (255). There is still romance within the economic framework that Mrs. Hedges builds on 116th Street, even if it does not conform to normative models of heterosexual coupling. Perhaps what emerges is a mutually beneficial deviance.

Petry's narrative prioritizes the experiences of a group of Black working women. First, the novel's brothel space invites reflection on those with limited autonomy and how they might provide a countermodel of belonging among Black women. Again, I do not want to suggest that Mrs. Hedges's brothel is utopic or outside capitalist exploitation. But I do want to suggest that Petry imagines the world of domestic labor in white homes as no less violent (recall the suicide at the Chandlers' Christmas, or the fact that her live-in domestic service work for the Chandlers plays a part in destroying Lutie's marriage and home). Second, the brothel space and its function carve out a different way to imagine comfort and community outside the normative and respectable. This aligns with *Monstrous Work and Radical Satisfaction*'s larger emphasis on Black leisure and sociality as indicative of monstrosity's productivity for Black women. So while the myths of financial sovereignty and body autonomy to which Lutie clings are illusory for urban Black working women during the 1940s, Mrs. Hedges and the wayward women surrounding her find, in the alternative economy of sex work, a modest way to live in the urban context. In contrast, Lutie attempts to find a way off the street by modeling herself after Ben Franklin or the Chandlers of Connecticut, but she still ends the novel a fugitive after killing Boots. Interestingly, though, flight and fugitivity might offer an opportunity not unlike the one Mrs. Hedges offers the women who work for her. Outside the law, propriety is no longer an option, and the path of ugly work is the only (but potentially liberating) path that's left.

Ultimately, what begins to emerge when one decenters beauty in *The Street* is another possibility for Black women's lives. Moving away from Lutie and her quest for the American Dream toward the alternative labor relations offered by Mrs. Hedges's brothel reminds us that the value of Black life and womanhood need not be measured by traditional beauty standards or commitment to American ideals, especially when those ideals are meant to exclude Black women. Understanding Mrs. Hedges as a potential model for a form of liberation is particularly important as readers watch Lutie end up on the lam for murder, forced to leave her son Bub behind as a ward of the state and juvenile delinquent. Petry reminds us that Black women and children suffer most profoundly in this American nightmare. The role of ugliness and ugly work are not just about appearance in Petry's novel but also about how Black women might name what American life does to them so that they are able to plot other courses.

Fugitive life is an idea and set of actions that Petry takes up in her young adult fiction, as well. Although it may seem odd to source Petry's representation of Harriet Tubman and even Tituba to a character like Mrs. Hedges from *The Street*, Petry's Mrs. Hedges can be read as a model of marginal and nonnormative Black womanhood, as the previous section of this chapter takes pains to illustrate. Mrs. Hedges, not Lutie, is the radical figure of the novel, and, thus, a

more influential model for understanding Petry's YA biographies of
Tubman and Tituba.

Historical Reconfiguration and Collective Action

If *The Street* was Petry's early claim to literary significance, it is her
young adult novels *Harriet Tubman: Conductor on the Underground
Railroad* (1955) and *Tituba of Salem Village* (1964) that constitute her
claim to Black cultural significance, as they do the work of instructing a next generation of young Black readers in what I perceive to be
radical satisfaction. Petry perhaps understood how essential stories
capable of instilling pride were to Black children after working in a
Harlem after-school program for latchkey children in the mid-1940s.
During this period of her working life, in which she also covered Harlem news for Adam Clayton Powell Jr.'s *The People's Voice,* she read
and did arts and crafts with the children of Harlem's working-class
residents and those living below the poverty line. Coming to know
the poverty of inner-city life, with which she had had no personal
experience before moving from Connecticut to Harlem, would alert
her to the needs of lower-income, Black, urban families in ways that
are easily traceable in her work—one need only think of the heart-
break that comes when reading of Bub's isolation while Lutie is away
at work in *The Street* (e.g., the stories he tells himself about the stray
dogs in the alley down below when he's home alone). I would argue
that these YA novels are an extension of Petry's desire to support and
influence the lives of working-class, urban Black women and young
people.

Moreover, these novels are part of a longer African American
progressive educational platform for young people that cultivates a
radical sense of self that is capable of countering American racism.
Harriet Tubman and *Tituba,* published between the Supreme Court
ruling in *Brown v. Board of Education of Topeka* and the Civil Rights
Act of 1964, highlight Black historical figures who embrace community organizing and use their imaginations to orchestrate Black
liberation amid white hostility and violence. Petry's YA fiction offers a continued charting of radical possibility for Black women and
girls, imbuing them with a sense of self-worth that has nothing to
do with American standards of beauty or racial assimilation. On the

contrary, a more pejorative understanding of ugliness—expressed through dread and horror—is turned back on the nation through these two texts.

Children's and young adult fiction are part of a larger tradition within Black literary production of recrafting the African American future by taking seriously the lives and literacies of Black children. As far back as the eighteenth and nineteenth centuries, Black writers and educators sought to provide countereducational materials to Black children and teens.[49] Katharine Capshaw and Anna Mae Duane remind us that, from the antebellum period into Reconstruction, to "imagine the black child as literate, upwardly mobile, and capable of inhabiting the same stories that were told to the future white citizens of the United States was to attack racial hierarchies at the root."[50] Likewise, the 1920s would find many of the major figures of the Harlem Renaissance (W. E. B. Du Bois, Langston Hughes, Nella Larsen, etc.) publishing children's texts, due both to "ideologies of progress" and increased "access to print venues."[51] One would imagine that by the mid-twentieth century the American imagination and educational system would have grown more robust, more capable of granting Black young people the right to age-appropriate stories centering self-worth and futurity. But the long-standing devaluing of Black children's lives in the United States continued to make such uplift and educational writing necessary. In her discussion of juvenile fiction and the literary left, Julia Mickenberg argues that from 1945 to 1965, "writers on the left taught children African American history in a way that implicitly challenged post-war racial hierarchies, communicated radical ideas about citizenship, and made a direct connection between past struggles against slavery and present struggles for civil rights."[52] The nation tarnished African American history so that it remained outside the scope of most of the U.S. public education system. Even when textbooks did include African American history, this history was diminished, or achievements were ignored for fear of losing Southern markets.[53] Mickenberg notes that by the 1940s, "historical inquiry among the left turned more and more to racial and ethnic minorities, as well as women, who had been left out even of anti-capitalist narratives of American history."[54] Petry is further tied to the radical literary left in her project of historical biographies for children and young adults.

Harriet Tubman is an icon in the long history of Black liberation and a favorite figure among Black writers and authors seeking to capture the imaginations of Black children.[55] From W. E. B. Du Bois's *Brownies' Book* to the premier issue of Paul Robeson's *Freedom* newspaper, Tubman's heroism was detailed on the page for young readers.[56] Ann Petry's 1955 biography of Tubman places her in league with the progressive (leftist) agenda of remedying the historical erasure of Black resistance to enslavement within the American educational system. Petry's narrative situates Tubman as doing the ugly work of rescuing enslaved people, which was, in the context of the slave system, illegal, physically uncomfortable, and mortally dangerous for all who embarked on the road out of bondage.

Petry's emphasis on Black young people's knowledge of Black history stands in stark contrast to the very first biography of Harriet Tubman, *Scenes in the Life of Harriet Tubman,* written in 1869 by Sarah H. Bradford, a white (former) abolitionist. Bradford opens her biography with the stated purpose of offering Tubman financial support so she might pay the mortgage on a small house she purchased for her parents after liberating them from bondage. The utilitarian motives for Bradford's production aside, the book's publication signals the limited financial benefit Tubman was able to receive from her clandestine labor during her lifetime. In her introduction to *Scenes in the Life of Harriet Tubman,* Bradford notes that unlike Harriet Beecher Stowe's *Uncle Tom's Cabin,* her narrative is not fictionalized: "The bare unadorned facts are enough to stir the hearts of the friends of humanity, the friends of liberty, and the lovers of their country."[57] Bradford was nonetheless aware of the racism of her potential reading public, anticipating that a book-length study of a Black woman would elicit contempt, especially because it makes "a heroine of a black woman, and a slave."[58] She writes Tubman as a heroine in spite of these predicted reservations from her readers.

But even as Bradford sought to craft Tubman as a heroic figure, years after emancipation and the end of the Civil War, Bradford's narrative disseminates the paternalistic discourse of abolition, making use of dialect prose to represent Tubman's voice and rarely critiquing white supremacy. Bradford also returns to the narrative conventions of the recently bygone slave narrative, particularly the authenticating documents: she included letters from other white former abolition-

ists attesting to the veracity of her narrative. These voices, also present in the body of the book, serve to legitimate Bradford's version of
the events of Tubman's life, which centers on Tubman's valor and her
need for charity.[59] There is also a letter from Frederick Douglass extolling Tubman. However, Douglass offers a perspective unlike the
many white men authenticating Bradford's rendition of Tubman's
life. He addresses himself directly to Tubman and thanks her for her
work toward Black liberation. He concedes that though she remains
less well-known and significantly less well-compensated than he, she
has been one of the most influential, fearless, and successful workers
for Black liberation.[60]

   Taken together, what emerges from Bradford's recounting and the
various testimonies is the story of a singular hero in Tubman. She is
a woman without measure, but she is also a woman without community, a woman of superhuman strength and cunning, and a woman
holding an unmatched commitment to ensuring the emancipation
of her family members and their closest friends, mostly. Very little of
the narrative captures the network of free and unfree Black people
with whom Tubman worked in order to ferry family, friends, and
strangers away from enslavement. Tubman as a "sagacious heroine"
emerges from the pens of Bradford and various others.[61] Rifle in
hand, the powerful, singular woman is what remains etched into the
imagination of many who have encountered Tubman from the nineteenth century to the contemporary moment.

   Less than a hundred years later, Petry's biography of Tubman
tells a story of a Black woman crucial to the liberation of a group
of enslaved people without relying on crafting her as a traditional
heroic figure. Petry imagines Tubman's heroism not as isolated but
precisely as initiated in and indebted to community. As Fred Moten
might say, Petry imagines Tubman as "radicalized in her singular-
ity."[62] This is to say, while Petry's Tubman is a powerful figure—even
as a teenager, Petry writes, Tubman is known for having "the kind
of courage rarely displayed by a grownup" (73)—she is also deeply
embedded in her community. Her young life is shaped by people
who are in constant conversation regarding their freedom, a group
with a collective quest for freedom: "This whispering about freedom, about runaways, about manumission, went on every night,
in windowless slave cabins all over the South. Slaves everywhere

HARRIET TUBMAN.

Mr. J. C. Darby, Harriet Tubman, 1868. Wood engraving on paper. Courtesy of National Portrait Gallery, Smithsonian Institution. Woodcut portrait is frontispiece in Sarah Hopkins Bradford's Scenes in the Life of Harriet Tubman *(1869).*

knew what happened in Washington, Boston, New York, Norfolk, Baltimore, if it dealt with the subject of slavery" (9–10). In this way, Petry establishes Tubman not as a singular heroic figure but as a person cultivated by her community and encouraged to undercut the plantation—the built environment and the ethos of violence and enslavement. For young readers, this community-centered heroine would model the valor of Black history as collective endeavor.

In addition to highlighting the collective work of the human community, Petry extends civic action to the larger natural world. The novel begins with an extensive overview of the Eastern Shore's topography, its flora and fauna. This topographical description has the effect of placing the natural world in opposition to the built environment of the plantation owned by Edward Brodas, the man who has enslaved Tubman's family and others. In laying out the plantation's dimensions and structures, Petry illustrates that the plantation is unnatural, marring the landscape. The natural world undercuts the plantation system: "The number of runaways from Maryland kept increasing. Especially from this Eastern Shore where the rivers and coves offered a direct route to the North, where the Choptank River curved and twisted in a northeasterly course, the whole length of the state—all the way to Delaware."[63] The unfolding of the sentence mimics the roll of a river. This technique suggests that running away is as natural as the river following its course. Likewise, Petry describes the enslaved people as "people who live close to the land" and who therefore measure time in a noncapitalist and nonindustrial fashion (4–5). This close association with the land is not a form of primitivism, for Petry, but a way of narrating Black liberation as inevitable, part of the world's natural order.

The natural world and the lives of the enslaved people form a connection that speaks to the enduring liberatory potential of both. For instance, in considering her work as a child born into enslavement, Harriet remembers herself as sensitive to the animal world: "She remembered how she hated the scaly tails of the muskrats, the wild smell of them, and yet did not want to find them caught fast in the traps" (72). This is not an explicit allegorical relationship between the nonhuman animal (muskrat) and the enslaved subject (Harriet), but it does register Tubman's sensitivity to care of the nonhuman world, or at least a desire not to do harm to it for the benefit of enslavers (an idea that is echoed in the work of Gwendolyn Brooks, as I argue in chapter 4). In this way, Petry illustrates what Tiffany Lethabo King theorizes as porosity, which works against the Enlightenment conceptualization of the body as "stable, autonomous, bounded, and separate from nature."[64] The porousness between the enslaved Black body, the natural landscape, and the nonhuman animal world ultimately allows Tubman to conduct her line of the underground railroad.

Written on the verge of the civil rights era and committed to building the historical significance of a key figure in Black history, Petry's *Harriet Tubman* introduces a new model of affirmation and collaborative action for young Black readers. Interestingly, Petry's narration is focused not exclusively on Tubman's heroic actions but also on the ways in which storytelling fortifies and uplifts the Black and enslaved community. We learn that after many successful rescues, Tubman develops a reputation, becoming a legend among the Eastern Shore's enslaved population. Stories are handed down about her "from one generation to the next, embroidered, embellished, until it would be impossible to say which part was truth, which part was fiction," always making the storyteller feel restored, if not mythically reified (129). However, what is striking about this heroic narrative is that in paying homage to Tubman, members of the community become weavers and storytellers in their own right. Petry's narrative refuses to make Tubman's quest for liberation singular, as well. She writes that many of the enslaved people "were afraid of the living death that awaited them in the rice fields, on the great cotton plantations, the sugar plantations, in the deep South—and so ran away" (9). Like Tubman, many other enslaved people engaged in the ugly work of resistance to remedy compulsory labor and death in bondage.

This emphasis on the power of storytelling is fleshed out even further as Petry closes the biography. She writes of Tubman's last years, spent selling vegetables door to door in Auburn, New York. Like the titular Mariner of Samuel Taylor Coleridge's "The Rime of the Ancient Mariner," Petry's Tubman is a weaver of tales, a master storyteller able to entrance her audience. In exchange for a cup of hot tea and butter, Tubman recreates the history of enslavement, her first trip to Canada, her time as a spy for the Union army, and her relationship to key figures in the fight for emancipation. She makes these stories come to life for her listeners. Petry describes Tubman's storytelling as a type of glamouring:

> Harriet and her one-woman audience were no longer in a quiet kitchen in the North; they were in cypress swamps, or walking under live oaks hung with Spanish moss that waved like gray drapery overhead; they saw cotton fields and rice fields, and heard the swash of a river against the banks, and listened to the aching sweetness of a mocking bird, on an island where an incredible moon turned night into day. (239)

The capacity to create the world anew for this small audience is a form of magic capable of instructing more deeply in the history of Black liberation. Like listening to the storytellers from back home, those listening to Tubman's tales are changed and fortified by her narrative. The transformative power of these stories speaks to the radical shift in cultural understanding and community bonding that Petry embarks upon in retelling Harriet Tubman's life for her young audience.

The role of storytelling as the ugly work capable of remaking one's world is a theme that Petry continues in her second young adult text. Nine years after publishing her Tubman biography, Petry published *Tituba of Salem Village* (1965). A bit over a decade earlier, Arthur Miller's *The Crucible* (1953) brought the Salem witches of the seventeenth-century Massachusetts Bay Colony to the American stage, reviving and revising the story for the mid-twentieth century. Miller is known to have written *The Crucible* as a commentary on the McCarthy era "witch hunts" against actors, journalists, government employees, and artists accused of being subversive due to their Communist Party affiliations or sympathies. Though she was not a member of the Communist Party USA, nor was she targeted by McCarthy, Petry's witch hunt tale tells the story of subversive community members from the perspective of the most marginalized among them: the enslaved woman Tituba Indian. Tituba was brought to the Massachusetts colony from Barbados, and Petry's fictionalization of the Salem witch trials explores the depths of depravity among these early settler-colonists. Additionally, the text illustrates how integral anti-Blackness was to colonial America.

Tituba opens in Barbados, situating the history of the Salem witch trials and colonial Massachusetts within the triangular trade. In fact, reorienting the story of the colony as bound to the West Indies has the effect of centering enslavement as part of early colonial American history. Like her literary ancestor Harriet E. Wilson, Petry counters historical narratives that locate Salem as an isolated community, untouched by the global economy of slavery. Instead, young readers get a historical intervention into the nation's origins meant to combat a national omission that leaves a character like Lutie with Ben Franklin as her role model. What if a young Lutie were able to look toward Tituba for her model of well-being in the world?

For instance, early in the novel, Tituba and her husband, John, are sold by their widowed mistress, Mrs. Endicott, to (real historical figure) Reverend Samuel Parris, so that the mistress can pay off a gambling debt. At the moment she learns her fate, Tituba imagines marooning herself and her husband on an island near Barbados.[65] Like the enslaved people in Petry's Tubman biography, Tituba imagines freedom but has no time to orchestrate the plan because Parris comes to retrieve her and John very soon after they are told they have been sold. In this early example of speculation, Petry lays the groundwork for Tituba's imagination as a potential source of escape and liberation. However, instead of time to escape, Tituba has time to realize the corruption of the white enslavers: "She sold us, not her rings or her necklaces, but her human jewels. She gambled us away. And cried about it afterwards" (37). She recognizes that her enslaver atomized her body for its value and then pretended to mourn her loss, as if atomization of the "captive body" can coexist with a heartfelt human connection.[66] The colony is embroiled in this atomization from the start of Petry's treatment. Again, this is important to the larger historical critique that Petry's work points to regarding Black women's marginalization within the nation.

In moving from Barbados to Massachusetts, then, the radical thread of Petry's retelling of the witch trials peels away from the various historical and fictional accounts of these events as part of some dark and anomalous chapter in American history. Instead, Petry asks her readers to question the very nature of good and evil, especially as the Salem villagers have defined the terms. Tituba looks at her hands and wonders, "Was this an evil hand," "a hand that wove and cooked and spun and cleaned and gardened, a hand that milked cows and nursed two children?" (172). This self-doubt produces incredibly powerful dramatic irony. In fact, the dread and horror Salem Village residents feel toward Tituba is called witchcraft, but it is actually rooted in her status as an enslaved person. For instance, as the accusations of witchcraft begin to circulate, her husband tells her she must stop talking to the animals that are in her charge because they appear to listen and take her direction. She responds by telling him everyone talks to animals. He goes on to note that the community believes she's a witch because the animals in her charge are never sick, always produce, and the garden she cares for is robust. She retorts: "I'm not a witch. How could I be a witch and not know it? I keep things clean for the animals, and I feed them. That's why everything seems to run smoother here. Hard work is what makes this place run smoother. Those farmer's wives could make their places run smoother if they did more work themselves. They leave everything to the bound girls" (187). Tituba resists being labeled a witch and instead sources the problems of Salem to the idleness of the landed residents and their reliance upon enslaved and bound (or indentured) labor. Tituba's husbandry skills and hard work become the ugly work that undermines the myth of the Puritan work ethic that circulates and is often weaponized against Black and other minoritized people in the United States.

Ugly work also gets practiced in the form of solidarity within Petry's text. Tituba's husband understands that the key to longevity for enslaved and bound people in this new world rests in refusal to participate in the witch hunt. When asked why he does not reveal the lies of an indentured worker, he says, "Because slaves and bound people do not tell tales on each other . . . because their lives are not their own. The people who own them do not protect them. No one protects them. And so they have to protect themselves and each other" (86). With the distance of history, young readers are encouraged to understand, as Tituba does, that idle hands and a dependency on enslaved labor are the real "witches" of Salem Village (176). The community's reliance on enslavement and servitude is a sin that the nation would carry into the nineteenth century. Like her portrayal of community in characters like Mrs. Hedges and Harriet Tubman, Petry's representations of Tituba and her husband highlight solidarity among the marginalized as the mode of both self- and community preservation.

Taking on the subject of witchcraft in Salem also offers Petry an opportunity to create a counternarrative regarding the power of Black storytelling and imagination as the ultimate form of ugly work. Tituba's ability to conjure her homeland through imagination becomes a mode of accessing liberation beyond time and place. Conjuring is particularly crucial if one remembers that Petry is retelling this story for young readers. While what happened in Salem is often framed as a crisis of faith or interpersonal grudges taken to their worst outcomes, Petry revises Tituba's role in the witch trials by sourcing them to a deep homesickness fed by collective storytelling. In various moments of the novel, we see Tituba "conjure" up Barbados in Abigail's and Betsey's minds, causing the latter to fall into a sleeping stupor (96). Likewise, Tituba realizes she can conjure an image of her home by looking at the drinking water in the livestock trough (106). In these scenes, we are prompted to think about the role of Black imagination and the societal response that seeks to pathologize and render it abject. When Parris beats Tituba for bringing bad luck into his home, she is deeply hurt in what she calls the flesh but also suffers an "unspeakable" injury of the spirit (194). Despairingly accepting her fate in the colonies, Tituba expresses a oneness with a broken-spirited horse, a beaten dog, and an enslaved person she once saw beaten in the cane fields of Barbados. But as the beating continues, her feelings shift. She confirms to herself that she is "a witch," if a witch is one able to travel home and imagine one's liberation. This moment of transfiguration—between abused enslaved person, animal, and witch—equalizes all those beings in ways that reorder the categories of human and nonhuman in profoundly complex ways. Again, this connectivity and porosity between the human and nonhuman worlds is similar to the technique Petry employs in her biography of Tubman.

Moreover, such play on language becomes essential as Tituba instructs John Indian on how to avoid being called a witch and linked to the imaginary "tall black man" who is supposed to be the devil bartering for the souls of the white girls of Salem (203). She understands that the whole ruse rests on the literalization of language, which does not have space for Black imagination. The fact that Petry imagines

Tituba as capable of breaching (early) American linguistic rigidity through imagination signals her progressive world-remaking: that Tituba can *imagine otherwise* is what is most frightening to the colonists. When Tituba signs her "confession," she admits to dealing with "the invisible world" (214). This invisible world is the world of imagination, and it allows her access to her homeland in the West Indies. Tituba conjures her satisfaction, her joy, despite the visible world of colonial America.

As I opened this chapter, I discussed the continued significance of Petry's best-selling novel *The Street,* which speaks across time regarding the economic and sexual violence that many members of the Black working class experience. In addition to these realities, many of Petry's Black women protagonists engage in the radical refusal of enslavement and liberal integrationism of the midcentury through practicing what I describe as "ugly work." From sex work to self-emancipation to witchcraft, Petry illustrates that what makes Black liberation so dangerous (ugly) to the status quo of the nation is its focus on collective action and the radical imagination. By refusing despair, rewriting history, and emphasizing the power of storytelling, Petry models for readers (young and adult) the importance of engaging in the ugly work of Black liberation.

· CHAPTER 2 ·

Home Work

Black Domestic Liberation

In a letter dated May 26, 1932, a twenty-four-year-old Dorothy West wrote to her friend and fellow Harlem Renaissance writer Langston Hughes, boldly declaring: "Lang, I love you. I'll never unsay those words as long as I live."[1] In March of that year, West and Hughes had embarked on a trip to the Soviet Union, along with twenty other African American writers, dancers, journalists, postal workers, college students, social workers, Communists, and activists. Amid the Great Depression, they were all more than happy to leave the United States to be paid to star in a Russian-written propaganda film that was to be called "Black and White," which explored Black and white worker solidarity in a Southern steel mill.[2] In her letter, West professes her undying love for Hughes, her desire for them to marry, and her vision of them having a child that would bind them together as a family. Though young, West was wise enough to understand that Hughes would be inclined to reject her proposal, so she tells him that after they conceive, he can continue his travels while she returns home to give birth. Simultaneously urging Hughes to take a risk and recognizing the foolishness of her proposal, West allows herself to imagine a future happy reunion between the well-traveled Hughes and his new family back in the United States. Her plan is both lovely and silly.

The love affair between West and Hughes was as disastrous as the film project they and their companions were in Russia to produce. Beyond infighting among the African American film-star hopefuls, the production company set to make "Black and White" produced a script treatment that Hughes declared improbable in its representation of African American and white laborers in the American South. Months went by; the Black Americans in Moscow had little to do besides enjoy the cultural exchange and the experience of being minor celebrities, a status they all acquired simply by being invited Black American "actors" in Russia. Many of them, especially Hughes, traveled throughout the Soviet Union and Europe. Though they never produced the film, and many of the Black Americans returned to the United States disgruntled, Dorothy West imagined that she had found love.

Love with Hughes, however, was as dubious as the trip itself. Hughes, handsome and flirtatious, was often insincere in his courting of women, according to Arnold Rampersad. Speculating on the reason Hughes (evidently) did not reply in writing to West's proposal, Rampersad writes: "[Hughes] knew he could not marry. Certain only of the solace of poetry and motion, he would not encumber himself."[3]

Arguably, though, West's letter reveals something more significant than her unrequited love for Hughes, as it represents an early iteration of West's creative thinking regarding courtship, marriage, and family—ideas that would shape much of her published writing during the 1930s and 1940s. In the letter, West appears to imagine the family anew for her life, which has radical repercussions for its expression in fiction. Within the span of only three and a half handwritten pages, West plots her vision of a future for two people as "full of vigor" as she and Hughes. West was perhaps no more sincere in her proposal to Hughes than he was in his flirtation, however. Because just as West was professing her undying love to Hughes, she was also falling in love with Mildred Jones.[4] While there is seldom a perfectly straight line from personal experience to creative output, West's international travels and love affairs may provide a portal of entry into her creative writings around romance and coupling.[5] More pointedly, West's time in Russia afforded her a deeper insight into romantic love's complexities; more practically, it gave her a financial cushion she could rely on as she worked to carve out a literary space for herself in the transitional decade bridging the Harlem Renaissance of the 1920s and the protest fiction era of the 1940s.

Moreover, West's emphasis on heterosexual coupling, marriage, and motherhood in her letter to Hughes highlights the options perceived to be viable for middle-class Black women in the early part of the twentieth century. In her 1992 canonical study on the

African American domestic novel, *Domestic Allegories of Political Desire*, Claudia Tate argues that post-Reconstruction Black women's novels are marked by a creative expression of the desire among Black women to attain their full citizenship rights. In Tate's view, domestic novels featuring Black courtship, marriage, and motherhood became sites of "private prosperity" and "civil justice" among postemancipation African American writers and readers.[6] Tate establishes the unique role of Black domestic novels in providing a pleasurable proving ground for recently emancipated Black women to formulate the full potential of their citizenship, to imagine and engage with political desires. Tate's work reminds us that these Black women writers advanced the marriage plot not to mimic Victorian-era "True Womanhood" novels but to write "novels about the moral development, spiritual maturation, professional aspirations, and economic advancement and of course social justice for Black Americans."[7] In her debut novel, *The Living Is Easy* (1948), Dorothy West takes the political aspirations of her post-Reconstruction precursors and remixes them to produce a critique of the possibility for heteronormative marriage plots to fully sustain Black women's aspirations in the early twentieth century.

Much like Ann Petry's use of the novel to critique norms of inclusion via beauty standards, West's fiction is filled with provocations around coupling and domestic configurations. West engages marriage and family through the domestic novel, turning toward the monstrous and ultimately testing the viability of female-centered Black domestic liberation. As I have laid out previously, the monstrous turn is best recognized as a shift away from characterizations, formalistic narrative structures and imperatives, and interpersonal relationalities meant to imaginatively remedy Black exclusion from the body politic under Jim Crow. I focus on the work done within the Black domestic space that has turned away from mainstream political desires for social and political integration. While West's work features elements of Black courtship, marriage, and family-making, she refuses their more "naturalized" outcomes, offering a countermodel of the sociality available to Black women.

A consideration of the Black household led by women is at the center of *The Living Is Easy*. West's attention to this women-centered

Black domestic space places her in conversation with the historical realities of Black domesticity postemancipation. It was through laboring in the service of the white household that many Black women secured financial stability and a future for their families. Attentive to the systemic racism of the labor marketplace, Saidiya Hartman notes that Black women had to "care for and replenish the needs of the white households" from enslavement to the Jim Crow period.[8] That said, she also reminds us that Black women's domestic and reproductive labor provided for the "endurance of Black social life," an idea I will revisit in my discussion of Alice Childress's work.[9] Langston Hughes's "A Song to a Negro Wash-Woman" (1925) captures this work and its outcomes:

> Yes, I know you, wash-woman.
> I know how you send your children to school, and high
> school, and even college.
> I know how you work and help your man when times are hard.
> I know how you build your house up from the wash-tub
> and call it home.[10]

Hughes's ode and Hartman's analysis pay homage to the Black home and the future-building made possible through Black women's labor and sacrifice.

But even as such domestic work provided for the endurance of Black social life, it has just as frequently been "blamed for its destruction."[11] American sociologists of the early twentieth century often set out to document living conditions and arrangements of Black people recently arrived from the rural American South to urban and northern locales. More often than not, they peddled a pathology narrative when describing Black women assuming head-of-household roles, often necessitated by economies established by racism and sexism. E. Franklin Frazier, who, in 1948 (the same year that West published *The Living Is Easy*), was the first African American to be elected to the American Sociological Society, devotes four chapters of *The Negro Family in the United States* (1939) to Black women's domestic leadership. Frazier ultimately pronounces this domestic model a "primitive" holdover from plantation life.[12] His tandem thesis is that patriarchal leadership among Black families produces not only modernity but also economic stability.[13] Those Black families living in urban poverty and experiencing social subjugation are "disorganized" because they fail to transcend this "backward model" of family formation. Likewise, about thirty years later, the U.S. Department of Labor's *The Negro Family: The Case for National Action* (1965), commonly known as the Moynihan Report (named for its author, then assistant secretary of labor and eventual Senator Daniel Patrick Moynihan), offers an expression of the national anxiety around the leadership of Black women. Moynihan's "tangle of pathology" discourse is now infamous in its critique of Black matriarchy as the source of what he also describes as Black "family disorganization."[14] Bookending West's novel, the work of Frazier and Moynihan marks the United States' sociological and cultural investment in developing and maintaining narratives seeking to control and pathologize Black women's labor and bodies.

In light of the long-lingering pathologizing of so-called Black matriarchy, it is important and valuable to consider the counternarratives that Black women have historically offered regarding their social marginalization. Toward that end, in this chapter, I offer insight into how Jim Crow racial politics are embodied and ruptured through queer reconfigurations of the Black home within West's *The Living Is Easy*. Coupled with her first novel, West's editorial work with her literary magazine *Challenge/New Challenge* offers a statement on radical writing, Black womanhood, and domestic satisfaction outside of heteronormality. Indeed, this chapter asks, in various iterations, if it is possible for Black women faced with de jure and de facto segregation, the threat of sexual violence, and gender inequality to find fullness by shaping the domestic space to their specific configurations, by centering their satisfaction. The satisfied Black woman is the monstrous figure that, all at once, refuses to be happy by conventional measures of society, spoils the happiness of those around her, and decenters white womanhood's capacity to set the dictates of proper femininity. The Black woman may be angry, she may be unhappy with the world as she experiences it, and she may be destructive in her tendency to live outside the norm. But what if she is also satisfied?

*Challenge/*ing the Black Left and
Reimagining Radical Politics

The line between the autobiographical and the creative is particularly permeable in Dorothy West's writing, so I place the novel into conversation with her Depression-era editorial work to better understand the political nature of domestic rupturing in a text like *The Living Is Easy*.[15] West used funds ($300) she netted from the Russian film company to seed the publication of a "little magazine" called *Challenge,* which she edited and ran for six issues between 1934 and 1937. Her editorial work illustrates her long-standing and complex relationship to the Black literary left, with her ambivalence around aesthetics and politics playing out in her work as editor of *Challenge.* Though framed as a writer of the middle class, I argue that West attempts to critique the limitations of leftist politics for Black women writers; she offers a vision of Black aesthetics that can foster radicalism within domestic and queer contexts. In this sense, the work of the domestic as West imagines it should not be dismissed as inherently apolitical. My aim is to encourage a reading of her more middle-class-oriented novel writing as part of a larger conversation about Black radicalism, and her editorial work is important to such a reading.

Challenge magazine began as a space for established and emerging Black writers to mingle. The first issue arrived in March 1934. It featured material from established writers of the Harlem Renaissance, namely Langston Hughes and Arna Bontemps, with a foreword written by James Weldon Johnson. In the first issue of the magazine, West outlines her editorial vision as bringing "prose and poetry of the newer Negroes" into the world.[16] However, West also proposes that the writers emerging in the magazine's pages might take up a challenge: to produce work that remedies the perceived failures of the Harlem Renaissance's "New Negroes," who "did not altogether live up to [their] fine promise."[17] She deliberately created a venue for Black aestheticians to cultivate and extend the unfinished business of the previous decade's literary potential.

Challenge magazine published writings that were attentive to aesthetics during a period in which an ideological orientation was taken by many to be a critical element of Black literary production. This ideological turn was due to a number of factors: the precarity of the Great Depression, a rise in anti-Black violence across the nation, and the increasing importance of Black cultural nationalism engendered by the influence of the Communist Party's "Black Belt" thesis, which argued that oppression of Black Americans within the United States marked them as a nation within a nation capable of self-determination, worthy of labor organizing, and politically significant.[18]

West's commitment to the magazine's aesthetic standards meant that she published fewer "emerging" writers than she might have hoped, however. In fact, in only the second issue of *Challenge*, published in September 1934, West addresses her readers with embarrassment regarding the shortage of quality submissions from younger writers: "We were disappointed in the contributions that came for the new voices. There was little that we wanted to print. Bad writing is unbelievably bad. . . . That largely explains why we are become a quarterly. We were just not ready to go to press at the end of a month. And we had to fall back on the tried and true voices."[19] Zora Neale Hurston, Countee Cullen, Arna Bontemps, Claude McKay, and "Mary Christopher" (Dorothy West's pseudonym while publishing in *Challenge*) account for a substantial portion of the content of this second issue.

West's commitment to aesthetic integrity in African American literary production was (and is still) often pitted against the political imperative of Black art in the 1930s. What surfaces in West's editorials (in columns beginning "Dear Reader") is the weight of placing a premium on aesthetics, which not only left her with few viable submissions to select from but also opened her to criticism from her more left-leaning contemporaries. Perhaps the tone was set in James Weldon Johnson's foreword to *Challenge*'s inaugural issue, in which he encourages emerging writers to avoid becoming "propagandists" and instead become "sincere artists."[20] By the time West published the fourth issue in January 1936, she was using her editorial space to explain and defend the magazine's seeming lack of a left-leaning political stance:

> Somebody asked us why *Challenge* was for the most part so pale pink. We said because the few red articles we did receive were not literature. We care a lot about style. . . .

We would like to print more articles and stories of protest. We have daily contact with the underprivileged. We know their suffering and soul weariness. They have only the meagre bread and meat of the dole, and that will not feed their failing spirits. Yet the bourgeois youth on the southern campus, who should be conscious of these things, is joining a fraternity instead of the brotherhood of serious minds. Leadership of the literate is infinitely preferable to the blind leadership of the blind.[21]

Again in her sixth issue, West makes clear that she will not let political viewpoint stand in for quality writing. She'd rather hold up her publication and wait for quality than diminish her vision in the name of the "correct" politics.

Lest it seem like West only criticized young Black writers, it is worth noting that she tried to encourage them, as well, by hosting a writing contest not unlike the *Opportunity* contest in which she had taken second prize only eight years earlier. In the March 1934 *Challenge,* West wrote that she was "rather pleased" with the issue, because most of the contributors were unknown, young Black writers.[22] She would work over the three years of *Challenge*'s publication to find and feature emerging voices that met her exacting expectations for carrying on the African American literary tradition.

West's literary work and personal life would again find themselves entwined as she closed the first volume of *Challenge* and began work on the second volume's first issue (Spring 1937). By late 1936, Dorothy West had begun a relationship with Marian Minus. West and Minus were probably lovers, and by 1937 the two women were living together with Marian's mother in New York City. The two would remain "close" until 1950.[23] Minus emerged from the Chicago South Side Writers Group, where she was a colleague of Richard Wright and other young Communist-leaning Black writers. Together these writers found an ideological space to hone their craft and develop an aesthetic vision of the role that literature might play in Black liberation. One can see Minus's literary and political influences on West's *Challenge* even before the two became coeditors of the short-lived *New Challenge* in 1937. For example, in what would be her final "Dear Reader" editorial for *Challenge,* West notes that nearly a year has passed since the last issue's publication and that this is "due to the lack of even fair material," which continues to confound her.[24] She expresses exasperation at the lack of collaboration with and quality submissions coming from her outreach to English departments at historically Black colleges and universities. She chides middle-class, college-educated readers with a pseudo-"Negro masses" argument:

> Our special hope is for the young Negro to grow to complete awareness of his heritage, his position as a member of a minority group, and his duty to take some active part in social reform. He must not escape, through his university training, to a consideration of himself as an entity apart. He must know the South, whose centre is not the campus. He must know the North, whose main stem is not Sugar Hill.[25]

The admonishment previews elements Richard Wright fleshes out in his influential essay "Blueprint for Negro Writing," which he published in *New Challenge* only a few months later (1937).[26] In this last "Dear Reader" column, however, West admits that she has "become greatly interested in a young Chicago group" (meaning the South Side Writers) and is publishing the work of a member of the group, Marian Minus, in honor of the group's promise.[27] At the same time, the South Side Writers' critiques of *Challenge*'s less-than-radical vision prompts West to offer them a special section in the magazine's forthcoming issue, so that "they may show us what we have not done by showing us what they can do."[28] This last issue of *Challenge* represents yet another transformation of West's life and literary vision.

By fall of 1937, West and Marian Minus shared editorial control of *Challenge*'s successor magazine, *New Challenge*, with Richard Wright listed as associate editor. Both Minus and Wright had ties to the Communist Party at that time, prompting most contemporary critics to argue that West had lost editorial control to the South Side Writers Group's proletarian vision. However, Cherene M. Sherrard-Johnson pushes against this standard reading of the editorial conditions of *New Challenge*, postulating instead that the "articles chosen present a productive tension that foreshadows the aesthetic debates about Black writing that occurred during the second Black Arts Movement in the 1960s and 1970s."[29] I would expand this observation to say that the tension among the magazine pieces can be seen in the editorial statement of *New Challenge,* as well. Lacking the humor and dialogic tone of West's "Dear Reader" columns in *Challenge,* the editorial statement makes clear that the plan for *New Challenge* is to increase the geographic scope of the contributors by soliciting writings from local writing groups nationwide, not unlike the South Side Writers Group, and to encourage these writers to produce works to and for the "Negro masses." However, the editorial also expresses pride in the magazine's political independence. The decision to maintain a subscription-based budget instead of receiving funding from a political organization was very important to West, who later in life declared that she never became a Communist because she was "too independent to be anything."[30] In this regard, the editorial statement of the *New Challenge* captures a respectful expression of warring ideas regarding the work of African American literature and the importance of artistic integrity at a crucial moment. The *New Challenge* folded after one issue due to lack of funding, but not before playing a part in solidifying the literary career of Richard Wright.[31]

West's self-characterization as an intensely independent thinker and her constant negotiation of aesthetics and politics during her *Challenge* editorial years led her to reject Marxism in her creative practice, though the trip to Russia and her "Dear Reader" editorials reflect West's investment in progressive Black politics. However, West remains best known for her novels depicting the so-called Black middle class. Critic Laurie Champion, for instance, asserts that *The Living Is Easy* and *The Wedding,* West's two best-known literary works, are populated by characters who are "undeniably upper-middle class."[32] West's wariness about the capacity of leftist ideology to maintain aesthetic integrity (so frequently on display in her editorial work), together with her critical reception as a chronicler of the Black middle class, would seem to suggest that her insights are applicable only to the lives of a privileged, politically conservative, and regionally specific segment of the African American population.

While there is no doubt that West's literary work is distinctive in its attention to class privilege and to a particular region of Black people that found little literary representation in the 1930s and 1940s—Black, middle-class New Englanders—to limit the work to only the "Black bourgeois" is to treat her work with a pejorative lens that misses the nuance of West's long-term vision. Applying a little pressure on the "Black middle class versus Black proletariat/ working class" divide that shaped much of the literary momentum of the 1930s and 1940s reveals more about a set of complexities in Black literary history than it might about class distinctions among Black Americans.

That is, the class divisions among African Americans have historically been more deeply rooted discursively than politically and socially, especially when one considers how wealth moves: intergenerationally. Most recently, Candice M. Jenkins has taken up the question of class differentiation and privilege within contemporary African American literature. Jenkins reminds us that while the Black bourgeois in the United States have more consistent access to capital and privilege, they inhabit flesh that is subject to the precarity of racial violence.[33] The performance of class privilege is often directly at odds with the performance of Blackness. And, as Jenkins points out, the "Black habitus" is most "precarious when it is accompanied by (or, perhaps, disrupted by) performances of class privilege."[34] Following Jenkins, I would argue that West is aware of the strivings of the Black bourgeois and the various threats the members of that community might face in the early part of the twentieth century. In fact, West's concern with the lives of "strivers and wannabes" offers a mediation between the Black proletariat and the bourgeois literary concerns that are often thought to be at odds in her time period.[35] Her works use genre to call attention to the volatility of class privilege among African Americans, reveal how normative class strivings remain out of reach, and suggest that conventional coupling is detrimental to Black well-being.

Until this point, I have approached West as engaged in a negotiation between (what she perceived to be) a cultivation of Black artistic integrity, on the one hand, and artless ideological expositions based in class and labor revolution, on the other. This dichotomy has shaped much of West's literary historiography. We see this more clearly in West's literary production and the long hiatus in her novel-writing career after the publication of *The Living Is Easy* (1948). West herself played into this particular narrative of her career when recounting the publication history of her second novel, *The Wedding,* which was not released until 1995. West explains the lag between her first and second novels as resulting from the ever-increasing Black cultural nationalism, fully fleshed out as the Black Power movement of the 1960s, or what West calls the "Black Revolution."[36] In a 1978 interview, West discusses having drafted fifty pages of a new novel (what would eventually become *The Wedding*) some years before, earning her a contract with Harper & Row. But, she confesses, she never delivered the novel for fear of it coming out in the wrong cultural atmosphere.[37] As Black militancy began to shape Black consciousness during the 1960s, West felt that her attention to light-skinned, middle-class Black people would garner rebuke: "They ran down every story that had to do with middle. . . . They hated the middle-class Black. And, of course, that's the point of my story."[38]

West's second novel takes as its central concern the lives of a highly privileged group of New England Black people who summer and marry on Martha's Vineyard during the civil rights era, a year before the *Brown v. Board of Education* (1954) landmark Supreme Court ruling. As Cherene M. Sherrard-Johnson notes, the "conflicts in *The Wedding* seem less urgent than the generational, transnational battles for civil rights and social justice. Indeed, West shared those concerns; they motivated her to suppress the novel until she could be reassured of a more receptive climate."[39] The 1980s renaissance of critical attention to the particularities of Black women's literary traditions and production ushered in a more capacious space for exploring Black life in literature. Black feminists and the scholarship they produced made it possible to turn critical attention to West's dynamic treatment of various gendered, sexual, and socioeconomic understandings of Black art and womanhood. In this way, her interest in Black class dynamics and gender and sexuality was better suited to the late rather than the mid-twentieth century.

West's troubled relationship with ideology and aesthetics, as witnessed in her editorials for *Challenge/New Challenge,* galvanizes something of what it means to attend to the domestic and social spaces of privileged and aspirational African Americans in the pre-civil-rights era. Perhaps the domestic novel's emphasis on the politics of home and hearth predisposes West's work to be taken as out of step with the politics of her contemporaries. Yet, there is room within our understanding of her domestic fiction to consider how she manages to create a radical vision for Black women's satisfaction, nonetheless.

Generic Deformation, an Additional Revolution

To get at the larger questions of class, race, gender, ideology, and genre as potential sites of intervention, it is important to turn to what West offers the novel of manners, in addition to her clear contribution to the domestic novel. I would argue that the two are linked subgenres; this is made evident in West's *The Living Is Easy*. West's approach allows her to critique both literary form and the form of the American nation as they relate to gender expectations and inclusion for Black women. In thinking of the class disunion characterized in *The Living Is Easy*, it is worth noting that she publishes the novel the same year Lionel Trilling's "Manners, Morals, and the Novel" appears in the *Kenyon Review*.[40] In his essay, Trilling notes that a "thick social texture" is usually associated with the British and Continental novel.[41] While he concedes that the twentieth century finds American society much thickened, he argues that "manners" remain poorly explored within the novel form among American writers. Identifying William Faulkner as the only contemporary American writer attentive to something akin to manners, Trilling ultimately rejects even Faulkner on the grounds that he is at a "disadvantage" because he is "limited to a provincial scene" (read: the American South).[42] Moreover, Trilling mentions the "Negro" only once, and one presumes he is alluding to Richard Wright's work, although the actual "Negro" remains unnamed in the essay's accounting for twentieth-century American writers of the social scene.[43] Unnamed and still mostly living and working in the South in the mid-twentieth century, Black Americans seem to have no place in what Trilling dubs the novel's capacity to capture "culture's hum and buzz of implication."[44] Trilling makes no mention of a minor Black woman writer like West. Yet, I believe the African American cultural "hum and buzz of implication" reveals itself through the thick social texture of West's representation of Black Boston.

If Trilling was unable to imagine Black manners, believing them

to be too parochial for literary treatment, the more significant problem of Black manners is that they are always already too political.
In *The Novel of Manners in America* (1972), a critical study of the
American novel of manners, James W. Tuttleton refuses to include
Southern writers, Jewish writers, or Black writers because "their
novels raise issues that transcend the question of manners and are
thus more intelligently discussed within other critical frameworks."[45]
Tuttleton's analytical discomfort with the inherent political significance of regional, racial, and ethnic literatures is clear in his assertion that when "political considerations . . . become obtrusive, not
merely a part of the fabric of the fictive social world, the novel becomes something other than a novel of manners—it becomes a radical or political novel."[46] The novel of manners goes astray if there is
too much admixture of political and ideological commentary. One
wonders what the ideological tipping point is that makes one novel
a "novel of manners" and another "radical." Perhaps it is a matter of
subtlety: critique without the appearance of dogma that might ruffle
the sensibilities of a (white) middle-class reader. Yet staying behind
the threshold of subtlety is a stifling restriction for writers seeking to
produce social commentary on the stakes and living conditions of
African Americans in the United States.

West's generic deformation is rooted in the necessary centering
of the Black experience within a novel of manners. She refuses to
lose sight of the Black character's coming to selfhood in a dynamic
and racially precarious society. *The Living Is Easy* explores the varied
layers of Black stratification when the structure creating differentiation (i.e., Black capital) is fundamentally unsound. Thus, the novel
of manners will always pose a problem for texts centering Black culture and characters. Black women are rarely alone together in fine
parlors where interpersonal cuts and slights are the height of one's
worries. The rude realities of Black life in America—from the brutalities associated with enslavement to the violence of racial oppression
postemancipation—do not lend themselves to a genre associated
with the gentle lives of middle- or upper-class white society. Yet,
Mary Sisney asserts that the Black novel of manners does exist and
that it has three fundamental and related concerns: "the fight for
acceptance, the loss of identity and the sense of oppression."[47] The
distinction between the early twentieth-century Black novel of man-

ners and its mainstream American counterpart is the former's emphasis on racial segregation.

The Living Is Easy concerns itself with manners in its commitment to exploring the social realities of how class ascendance is achieved, maintained, and lost by African Americans just one or two generations removed from either servility or enslavement. So while she situates the majority of the novel's action in Boston, there are flashbacks of Cleo Judson's life in South Carolina as a young girl. In this way, West reminds readers that African American manners are subjected to and formed around a broader national character shaped by the afterlife of slavery; they are eternally both political and particular. The varieties of family success and precarity that concern West are inherently particular to those persons subjected to American racialization and anti-Black violence. West's cynical approach to upward mobility and the stability of class ascension for Black people is sharpened by the social realities laid bare in the novel of manners. Still, West could not take for granted what Henry James and Edith Wharton took for granted: the hunger among readers for stories about "old money," long-standing American families, European tours, and the minor disputes between the established monied families and social climbers. That is to say, while there might be social climbers and monied Black people, a lack of guaranteed intergenerational wealth is not merely an individual trouble.

Black wealth and its lack takes on the shape of a systemic concern for the Black family of means in *The Living Is Easy*. The novel's narrator discloses that Black Bostonians "were not a privileged group, that no Negro was immune from the white man's anger when he did not watch his step. These self-styled better Negroes were standing still, sticking their heads in the sand, pretending that liberalism was still alive in Boston. They were using the transplanted Southern for their scapegoat" (131). This passage illustrates the fact that class uplift cannot protect Black persons from the violence of American manners and that a "respectable" set of behaviors will never deliver Black characters from oppression. One is reminded again of Candice M. Jenkins's notion of the precarity inherent in the Black bourgeois performance of class privilege. West's contribution to the novel of manners rests in her deformation of the genre's core intention of delineating cultural differences between classes and the social relations that maintain those distinctions without an implicit critique of the core structural inequities inherent in American society. Ultimately, she ties the societal to the familial through the domestic novel.

Matriarchy Is the Message

Thus, there are many ways to understand Dorothy West's work as disruptive and typical of Black women's refusal of racialized gender expectations within the early decades of the twentieth century. In their introduction to *Where the Wild Grape Grows,* Verner D. Mitchell and Cynthia Davis suggest that West's writing focused on "dysfunctional marriages based on hegemonic definitions of beauty and success."[48] It is West's attention to dysfunction implicit in the hegemony of marriage and beauty for African American women that I argue marks her writing as an early harbinger of many of the ideas that became central to Black feminist criticism of the post–civil rights movement of the 1970s and 1980s. Beyond presenting us an opportunity to consider feminist motifs within the text, *The Living Is Easy* does the more radical work of centering relationships among Black women that have the potential to reconfigure the ways we understand and value the workings of Black domestic spaces. Cheryl A. Wall argues that Black women's writing about family is always a challenge to "the structures of patriarchy; they mainly reject heterosexism, and they usually oppose nationalist ideologies. For the most part, [Black women writers] invoke metaphors of the family to revise the meaning of family."[49]

Returning to the letters West exchanged with Hughes while on the Russia trip, we recall that she attempted to revise the notion of the family even within her imagined, otherwise heteronormative romance. Extending Wall's observations regarding the family in the hands of Black women writers, we are encouraged to imagine Black domestic spaces that rupture domesticity and conventional notions of familial happiness. I signal another set of possibilities for Black domestic sociality that relinquishes all adherence to normative modes of romantic partnering, household configuring, procreation, and inclusion within the affective community of domestic happiness.

Essential to my argument for the remainder of this chapter is an examination of the movement away from the patriarchal family romance toward which many African American women writers strove during the twentieth century. In West's *The Living Is Easy,* we can see how turning away from domestic happiness produces monstrous ends. The third-person novel features one of the most unconventional protagonists in African American women's literature: Cleo Judson. The light-skinned, green-eyed Cleo is manipulative, greedy, and sexually withholding—and those are among her better qualities. In fact, in the opening scene of the novel, readers are introduced to Cleo through the contents of her pocketbook: a cloth square filled with talcum powder; a lollipop to quiet her daughter, Judy; an Irish-linen handkerchief, for style; a square cotton hanky, for cleaning up Judy when she gets sticky; "a change purse with silver, half of which Cleo, *clandestinely and without conscience,* had shaken out of Judy's pig bank"; and forty-five dollars she came by "more or less legitimately" from tricking her husband.[50] This collection of objects speaks to Cleo's character as a mother to her only child, Judy, and as a partner to her husband, Bart Judson. Bart (a.k.a. the Banana King), a Black entrepreneur and fruit grocer in Boston, serves from the very opening paragraph as a foil to Cleo's worst character flaws. Where Bart is generous, she is stingy, and not just with money but also with attention and familial love. Ultimately, Cleo's greed, lack of conscience, single-mindedness, and desire to accumulate wealth at all costs—even if it means cheating her husband and daughter, and later other family members, out of their futures—mark her as perpetually out of step with the idealized domestic that Tate traces in *Domestic Allegories of Political Desire.* Instead of the proper aspirational domestic idealization of gender roles or a domestic plot that relies on "a tradition of politicized motherhood" and maternity "as instruments of social reform," West crafts a heroine intent on usurping head-of-household status and wielding it in service of her vision.[51]

Moreover, Cleo's refusal to adhere to patriarchal domination is perhaps what makes her a monster to those in her orbit. For instance, during an argument with her husband, she nonchalantly dismisses his requests for her honesty by telling him, "Don't try to make me over" (151). Cleo will not be changed by any man; instead, she flees from Bart's love (81). While the other women in her family happily show love to the men in their lives—husbands, fathers, brothers, cousins, and even strangers—Cleo despises men for no reason other than this: "Men were her enemies because they were men" (38). Man-hating aside, it is useful to consider Cleo an early Black feminist. To this point, Mary Helen Washington notes that *The Living Is Easy* contains an array of feminist themes: "The silencing of women, the need for a female community, anger over the limitation and restriction of women's lives."[52]

What marks Cleo as particularly monstrous is her refusal to represent domestic bliss and romantic coupling. In this way, she predates the feminist figure that Sara Ahmed describes as the "killjoy." More than merely noting their suffering under the "happy house-wife" ideal, Ahmed historicizes the instrumentalizing of women's happiness, its construction as conditional upon the happiness of another (typically parents, husband, children), which is always asymmetrical in its reciprocity.[53] Thus, Ahmed's feminist killjoy is the woman set free by her imagination, liberated from happiness, able to articulate desires that emanate outside the happiness of others, and, most important, committed to "'spoiling' the happiness of others."[54] Additionally, Ahmed links the feminist killjoy figure to the Black feminist tradition of Audre Lorde's and bell hooks's "angry Black woman" figure: "The angry Black woman can be described as a killjoy; she may even kill feminist joy, for example, by pointing out forms of racism within feminist politics."[55] I would assert that Black women's inherently antagonistic relationship to social and political norms is affectively more dynamic than mere anger can capture. Depicting the Black woman as angry is one mode of representation, but I seek to expand the affective registers available to Black women so that it might include what I call satisfaction.

Cleo is a figure that forgoes conventional notions of happiness in favor of a domestic world of her devising. To get there, she spoils the happiness of most of those around her, offering a version of unhappiness she has chosen just for them. The novel relates Cleo's tendency to actively refuse to conform to normative modes of supposed respectability mandated for a Black woman seeking upward mobility in the mid-twentieth century. For instance, when Cleo reads aloud Louisa May Alcott's *Little Women* (1868), she delights in hearing her voice and losing herself in the novel's attention to a time and place devoid of patriarchal authority. Already we witness Cleo's satisfaction as an insult to the gender and class expectations that relegate working-class Black women to particular forms of silence and submission. One can imagine that Cleo thinks herself a "Jo," like the many readers who have come to Alcott's novel across generations. Like Jo, Cleo is forced by her very womanhood to disavow independence in favor of security in a patriarchal world. Cleo's mother, seeing what she understands as "wildness" and fearful that Cleo "might disgrace herself" with "wantonness," sends her away from her childhood home as a form of insurance against budding sexuality (24). While Alcott's Jo finally finds a voice within her creative world, Cleo lacks an artistic form. In this way, she is more like Toni Morrison's titular Sula: dangerous.[56] A precursor to Sula, one chained by social expectations of Black bourgeois propriety, Cleo marries but refuses marital happiness. She instead opts to mold her life's trajectory (and that of the other women of her family) against heteronormative, nuclear family structures, even while she occupies the role of wife and mother.

The excess and anxiety surrounding Black female autonomy are indicative of more extensive critiques regarding womanhood and gender roles explored in *The Living Is Easy*. Again, we see this sort of critique of the limits placed on female autonomy when Cleo considers what it means to be gendered male: "What was there to being a boy? What was there to being a man? Men just worked. That was easier than what women did. It was women who did the lying awake, the planning, the sorrowing, the scheming to stretch a dollar. That was the hard part, the head part. A woman had to think all the time. A woman had to be smart" (21). Cleo's views on men do not suggest much respect or sympathy for them. But she sees clearly that patriarchal power is constructed at the expense of women's power and autonomy, and this is decisive for her. At the core of Cleo's monstrousness, then, is a bold, critical, and steadfast refusal to accept the authority of men simply because they were assigned male at birth and are thus able to access manhood and patriarchal privilege.

Notably, this critique of masculinity and men does not necessarily increase her sense of the value of the women in her life; Cleo's critique of the inherent inequity of patriarchy is not an automatic articulation of a broad feminist ideology. Instead, her gender animus opens up a space for critical evaluation of unearned male privilege that Black bourgeois romance and filial plots often occlude. Through Cleo's hostility, we can begin to deconstruct the nuclear family romance, a project vital to Black upward mobility and to putting an end to the pathologizing of Black families.

Rejecting the romance of post–Jim Crow integration and upward mobility can mean rejection of normative womanhood. In this way, Cleo's distaste for the white women in her life nearly matches the contempt she has for men. For instance, when she first moves north from South Carolina, she does so as a ward of Miss Peterson of Springfield, Massachusetts, and then Miss Peterson's friend in Boston, Miss Boorum. Though officially categorized as a dependent of both women, Cleo recognizes herself as a servant. In this way, readers must question the sort of sociality possible between Black women and white women. Cleo understands that she and the white women relate to one another through identities scripted by long histories of race and gender relations. This is a lesson she was beginning to learn back in South Carolina when she was forced by convention to "put on a long dress," tie up her long hair in a bandanna to cook in other women's kitchens, and address her childhood friend Josie as "Miss Josephine" (24). By the time Cleo becomes the ward of these older white women, she recognizes them as nearly indistinguishable caricatures of antebellum-era white mistresses: "One old white woman looked just like any other old white woman to her. Only difference was Miss Boorum wore false teeth that slipped up and down when she talked" (27). Motivated by an inverted sense of racial fungibility, Cleo is merely in a state of "suspension" until she might run away, leaving a "sassy note saying, Thank you for nothing. Good-bye and good riddance. If I never see you again, that will be too soon" (28). Again, Cleo has a sense of herself as valuable beyond what is ascribed to her by white womanhood.

Eventually, she meets Bart Judson and steals away as she planned—through marriage. Cleo's act of defiance, this fugitive refusal, rebuffs the romance of allyship and care that Miss Peterson and Miss Boorum pledge to give. (They send money to her mother monthly with notes describing Cleo's good deeds, as if that serves as adequate compensation.) Cleo appears to understand what theorist Christina Sharpe expresses in the form of a question: "How can the very system that is designed to unmake and inscribe her also be the one to save her?"[57] In light of systemic neglect posing as salvation, West's characterization of Cleo's lack of gratitude to these white women reveals their inability to care for her outside limited social scripts and long-standing controlling images of Black womanhood.

Ruses of Seduction

More insidious than sexism and white supremacy is the commingling of these two as a mode of endangerment to Black womanhood. The white women characters in *The Living Is Easy* practice a form of benign neglect that puts Cleo at considerable physical risk. This risk takes the form of Miss Boorum's nephew, who lusts after Cleo with a desire he thinks is rooted in his loins but is grounded in his awareness of the long-standing American myths and scripts about Black women's lust and availability. It seems important to note that the nephew has no proper name (he is "Miss Boorum's nephew"), so we are forced to always consider him via Miss Boorum. This suggests that white womanhood and white masculinity are both implicated in Black women's sexual and physical endangerment. In fact, not giving the nephew a name prompts the reader to see him, the sexually predatory white man, as a kind of (literally) nameless peril inflicted by a white woman (Miss Boorum) on a Black woman who works in her home (Cleo). The most treacherous element of Miss Boorum's nephew's priming and perversion is his sense of his own helplessness to prevent himself from assaulting Cleo: "He was seduced by her chastity. He would never be free so long as he knew he could be her first lover. Until he could see the face of her purity replaced by the face of surrender, her image would lie on his lids to torment him" (30). Miss Boorum's nephew gifts Cleo a bicycle with "the bloody hope that she would break every bone in her body and destroy her beauty, if not herself" (31). The nephew, lingering in slavery's afterlife, models the sort of "confusion between consent and coercion" that Saidiya Hartman points to as the "discourse of seduction" so familiar to the plantation racial-gender logics.[58] In the novel's case, the nephew's ruse of seduction allows him to displace his desire onto Cleo and thus hold her responsible for any violence that befalls her at his hands. What is convincing about West's construction of this characterization of white masculinity, one of the few that the novel represents, is the way it calls attention to the material endangerment posed by masculinity and whiteness. Indeed, what may first appear to be general misandry on Cleo's part must be read as resistance to gendered and race-based threats to her well-being.

The appearance in the story of the bicycle signifies the arrival of mobility, a concept that is particularly fraught within *The Living Is Easy*. Cleo's movement from South Carolina and the masses of Black Southerners arriving to and reshaping the residential landscape of Boston remind readers that the novel is at its core a migration narrative. Thus, Miss Boorum's nephew's gift of a bicycle might seem to hold the promise of delivering Cleo a means of escape. When she mounts the bicycle, Cleo is impervious to the possibility of danger because she "still did not know there was anything she was incapable of doing" (31). That "still" here suggests, however, that there is a real alternative to Cleo's self-regard that will divest her of her hubris. That reality comes in the form of her future husband, Bart Judson, into whom she "unromantically" runs while biking. In this sense, the bicycle, destroyed by the impact of Cleo's and Bart's bodies, serves as the vehicle for delivering her from one patriarchal context to another, highlighting the limits of mobility for Black women in the early part of the century.

Thus, in a world set to variously neglect, lust over, pander to, or control her, Cleo's self-directed aim is to find a mode of being amid the abjection and relative immobility that results from her race and gender. Monstrousness—behaving out of line with social scripts and refusing normative affective relationships—offers her a method of achieving freedom within her unfreedom. She lives a sort of stolen life, in Fred Moten's sense: "Stolen life," Moten writes, "disorders positive value just as surely as it is not equivalent to social death or absolute dereliction."[59] The narrator notes that Cleo learns to be neither good nor bad as she enters into adulthood: instead, she decides to engage the world through guile (28). Taking a cue from Paul Laurence Dunbar's collective first-person speaker in "We Wear the Mask," Cleo's characterization represents a version of Black womanhood that exists within the structures of normativity (marriage, family, sexuality) while refusing to allow those structures to govern her personhood.[60]

One of the most compelling forms of refusal on display in *The Living Is Easy* is observable within the text's morphing of the heteronormative marriage plot. Cleo's husband, Bart, is twenty-three years her senior and is the owner of a successful fruit grocery in Boston. Both Cleo and Bart are transplants from the American South, him born under enslavement in Virginia and emancipated before his first birthday. They both value property and the accumulation of wealth: Bart because he is committed to notions of what it means to be a provider for his family and Cleo because, though married, she desires to ensure her independence. Bart and Cleo live in a nearly sexless marriage: Bart notes that he can count on one hand, and have fingers left over, the number of times she's allowed him to have sex with her. We learn that Cleo, in turn, doesn't have any sexual hang-ups. Instead, Cleo practices near-celibacy during her decade-long marriage because she refuses the implication, inherent (in her view) in the expectation of sex in marriage, that "she was incomplete in herself" (36). Cleo's refusal of the reproductive functionality expected of someone gendered and socialized to be a woman provides much of the tension in the early chapters of the novel. For example, Cleo allows Bart to believe she's pregnant with a second child (a son) to manipulate him into supporting her scheme to rent a larger home that will lodge her sisters and their children (a different sort of growing family). The demand that femininity accommodate patriarchal visions of the nuclear family is distorted under Cleo's guidance.

Cleo refuses the idealization of "Black domesticity" that Tate outlines in *Domestic Allegories of Political Desire,* an idealization offered to bourgeois Black women postemancipation as they attempted to negotiate their roles with the hopes of national assimilation. Toward this end, Ann duCille points out, "Cleo would be *king,* not mother."[61] I would go a step further and suggest that "wife" is the role Cleo least desires. The distinction rests in Cleo's refusal to subordinate herself to her husband's well-being, refusing to take the role of a domestic helper. Cleo rejects his rendition of Black domesticity. The inherent rub of Cleo's autonomy is that it has little to do with Bart. Attributing her dissatisfaction to some shortcoming of Bart's constitutes a misreading of the significance of Cleo's pitting of her will against his. Such personalized opposition would limit the novel's thematic arc to a traditional battle of the sexes, which it is not. Bart has no desire to control Cleo; he is instead a patient cultivator of growing things. So when the text describes Cleo and Bart's "sex battle" beginning when she turns twenty, it means that they have conflict surrounding her sexual autonomy (35). Faced with her sexual withholding early in their marriage, Bart believes he will wait for Cleo with "love and patience," because there is "satisfaction in seeing it ripen" (35). In fact, Bart loves his fruit nearly as much as he loves his wife. Fruit and wife become fetish objects within the affective and financial economy of the text, with Bart obligated to care for both. In this way, I am convinced that West's narrative opens up space for sexlessness within marriage as a way for a Black woman to express a viable form of satisfaction.

Following this turn to imagining satisfaction that might come through heterosexual marital sexlessness, I would conjecture that what is at stake in Cleo's refusal is another form of family formation, that of a queer family, that places the novel outside the bounds of the traditional expectations of the domestic novel. Falling more in line with Hortense J. Spillers's thinking regarding possibilities available to Black people through the gender "unmaking" devised with the body theft of enslavement, the novel registers as an early Black queer domestic novel.[62] Let me clearly state that I am not making the argument that *The Living Is Easy* is an early lesbian novel. First, the book revolves around a heterosexual marriage plot, and the women-centered family structure that comes to displace the heteronormative nuclear family is one based in biological kinship (sisters)—any love there is in the novel is filial. As Ayesha K. Hardison notes, Cleo privileges "being a sister over being a wife" and thereby "restructures heterosexist foundations of domesticity in her female-centered household."[63] Likewise, Verner D. Mitchell and Cynthia Davis note that West never wrote about "homosexuality." Still, her writing is rife with couples "who sacrifice love for marriages of convenience based on socially sanctioned attributes such as color and class," and this "reflect[s] a dynamic that West would certainly have understood in terms of the risks of 'coming out' to family and friends."[64]

Second, it is not necessary to pin down West's sexual practices in order to discern and theorize the criticisms of heteronormative marriage (and the general misandry) that emerge in the novel. West's work, published amid the post-WWII entrenchment of the nuclear family, is exemplary of a critical attempt to consider alternative forms of Black women's family-making. Her work stands as an early example of how Black women's narrative work might require a more expansive window for reading ideological interventions. This is particularly important in light of the tensions that I outlined in the publication history of *Challenge/New Challenge*. Of course, West wrote before the unified and articulated Black feminist political project codified. She would have been unwilling to identify as a lesbian in the postwar, pre-Stonewall era. Thus, queering the novel allows for a different form of radical gender and nonnormative heterosexuality politics to emerge. In this sense, Cleo is a "woman monster" in terms of the text's overarching perspective: she is the Black feminist killjoy because she draws attention to the limits of heterosexual romantic love in crafting a sense of family and autonomy for Black women.[65] Indeed, early in the novel, West twice employs some variation on "monstrous" to describe Cleo (30, 77). The narrative, unable to maintain a generosity toward Cleo's narrative perspective, seems to reduce her actions to mere cruelty and ambition. Following the conventions of the domestic novel, which must punish Cleo for her monstrous behavior, she "is punished with the ultimate loss in patriarchal culture: She is left without a man."[66]

While it is true that as the novel ends, Cleo is without a husband and looking toward her nephew as the next generation of man who might worship her, I believe she is not looking for power over male figures, neither companionship nor even adoration. Thus, more than modeling the domestic novel that Tate argues was the hallmark of Black women's aspirational literary production, West's work is a deconstruction of the domestic novel's ability to affirm heteronormative, nuclear belonging for the Black family. As I stipulated in my introduction to this book, West joins a group of Black women writers for whom generic innovation is a form of aesthetic self-articulation. West produces, then, a narrative intervention into Black queer family-making before such identification was imaginable and possible, using elements of a genre meant to affirm the normative family model. *Queer*, for my purposes, takes on the connotation of atypical and nonnormative modes for valuing and understanding Black kinship structures. I arrive at this meaning via Cathy J. Cohen's canonical theorization of *queer*. For Cohen, more than a sexual orientation, queerness can be a mode of coalition-building among marginalized groups committed to liberation. Moreover, Cohen articulates *queer* as a political project that is capable of harboring "heterosexuals on the (out)side of heteronormativity."[67] Resisting the dichotomy of straight versus nonstraight, Cohen's reasoning places intersectional politics above singular identity configurations that may not necessarily challenge power structures. Cohen reminds us that poor Black women, "lacking power and privilege, although engaged in heterosexual behavior, have often found themselves outside the norms and values of the dominant society. This position has most often resulted in the suppression or negation of their legal, social, and physical relationships and rights."[68] This intersectional approach allows *queer* to signify beyond sexual practice, to allow those marked as marginal to normativity to stand in a more formidable minoritized community. In this sense, *The Living Is Easy* functions more as an early Black queer domestic novel, as it features both asexuality and same-sex family-building. The novel additionally features an early African American literary treatment of compulsive eating and body shaming.[69]

A capacious queer lens allows us to think of an art able to capture the contradictory and compelling work of the family, gender, and Blackness. An elastic understanding of Black family formation, more importantly, invites a consideration of intimate relationships and a domestic space built on Black refusal. In *The Living Is Easy,* we see Cleo's narrative arc freed from the romance plot typically associated with the domestic novel, which opens the text to other forms of family formation beyond the cispatriarchal heteronormative. The female-centered Black household comes into view. While Meredith Goldsmith posits that "sororal bonds mirror heterosexual bonds in their disparity of power" in the novel, I would argue that we should think a bit more critically about the way power functions and that it is Cleo's "monstrosity" that renders her at odds with her sisters.[70] There is no doubt that Cleo's story arc entails her outlandish quest for power and control over her sisters. Still, I believe it is because she sees the effect of broader systemic inequities that have bound each of these Jericho women to both the patriarchy and the burden of American racism.

Focusing on systemic inequality, embedded in Cleo's combative relationship with her husband—and all men, for that matter—is shrapnel from relationships formed in a history of domination reaching as far back as enslavement. While scholar Jennifer M. Wilks argues that we see in Cleo the grasping toward some "New Black

Womanhood," I would suggest that lingering slave relationships provide another mode for understanding Cleo.[71] We might read Cleo's desire to maintain her own physical and financial autonomy within the confines of her marriage against a backdrop of the scenes of subjection that mark Black women's sexual history as perverse. There is a way to read an idea of Black women's self-sufficiency against multiple grains: against the grain of the period's notion of cisheteropatriarchal Black domesticity as key to national inclusion, but also against contemporaneous critiques of capitalism that prompt us to read Cleo's acquisitional impulses as unmooring her from a more progressive logic.

Regarding this latter concern, Cleo's greed emerges as an important element of her power. As a Black female character, Cleo's desire for autonomy and her unyielding quest to reconfigure her entire living matrilineal family under her roof is indicative of her yearning to live outside the tyranny of the master–slave dialectic. In this case, Bart becomes a (misidentified) stand-in for a member of the master class due to his gender and his financial capacity to enact Cleo's subordination. At no point does Bart wield this potential power, but Cleo lives in expectation of such a subordinating relationship because she occupies the role of wife/woman. Cleo thus assumes and maintains a combative stance throughout the narrative: "She would show Mr. Judson that she could take a house and be its heart. She would show him that she could bend a houseful of human souls to her will. It had never occurred to her in the ten years of her marriage that she might be a helpmate. She thought that was the same thing as being a man's slave" (71). "In classical contract theory, then, the wife is the analog of the servant, and marriage the analog of the wage relationship," Amy Dru Stanley asserts.[72] Likewise, Cleo perceives within the heteropatriarchal confines of marriage the potential for a type of servitude. Her resistance to traditional marriage roles is exacted in the limited physical and psychological intimacy she acknowledges and allows between herself and Bart.

Instead of heteronormative partnering, Cleo's understanding of power and autonomy is embedded in her enslaved foremothers' refusal of racialized and gendered subordination. That might seem oxymoronic considering the totalizing terror of the plantation system. Cleo's matriarchal narrative is one that highlights a type of autonomy within a system that reduces Black bodies to the status of property. I want to quote at length Cleo's ruminations about what she will tell Judy of her foremothers:

> Great-aunt Fanny who hung herself in a hay loft where her master left her running blood after he gave her first whipping for stepping on the tail of his valuable hunting hound. She was her master's whelp, too, but she wouldn't take a whipping just because she was a mongrel. And great-grandmother Patsy—the time Old Missus scolded her for burning biscuits, the only time she ever burned an old pan of bread in forty years of baking, Great-grandmother Patsy walked out of the kitchen and down to the river. When they fished her out by her long Black hair, her soul had got free and she didn't have to listen to anybody's life forever after.
>
> The old-time Jericho women lived proud as long as they could. When they couldn't live proud, they preferred to die. Not one of them was born to take anybody's lop or anybody's lash. When Judy was ready to know about slavery, these were the tales to tell her. (90–91)

These remembrances illustrate Cleo's overarching relationship to slavery and her imaginings of how she might pass on to her daughter a link to freedom that resides even in that unfree state. As Cleo recalls it, the Jericho women would die rather than live without pride.

Moreover, this family lore captures the atrocities of white power, which disciplines Black people at a whim. Cleo's understanding of Black women's influence in the face of white indifference is one that expresses itself through acquiring the property of others: in this case, one's own enslaved body, and doing with it what one will. Thus, it is not a death wish that Cleo wants to pass down to Judy but rather a willingness to put her body on the line for passions and desires that run counter to the establishment. Cleo's family lore captures impulses to document resistance to the master–slave dialectic through counternarratives of Black female solipsism, a refusal to remain owned by or indebted to white people.

If satisfaction has among its many meanings the repaying of debt, what the Jericho women illustrate is the capacity to claim their bodies, their labors, their histories away from the white household, which held them in bondage. Moreover, Cleo's commitment to the stories of her matrilineal ancestors reveals an understanding of the unrealistic cultural presumption of Black women's indebtedness to white supremacist, heteropatriarchal systems. Of course, as Saidiya Hartman notes, emancipation may have ended chattel slavery in the United States, but it did not "mark the end of bondage. A free(d) individual was nothing if not burdened, responsible, and obligated."[73] In this way, Cleo and the women in her family attempt to exist within their value system, which is inherently at odds with the national valuation of enslaved people and their progeny for generations to come. This is not naturally a generative model of resistance, but it does offer a counternarrative to the limiting national logics that continue to imagine Black women as property. It provides a model of divestment from white supremacist, patriarchal, sexist systems of subjection.

West's novel, published nearly two decades before Senator Moynihan's *The Negro Family: The Case for National Action,* anticipates critiques of Black women's desire and aptitude for household leadership in the late twentieth century. In contrast, West offers an alternative and vexing imagining of Black matriarchy via Cleo's quest to unify all the women of her family under one roof and recreate her Southern childhood. The question, then, becomes how we might read Black maternal solipsism as a form of Black satisfaction that has the potential to reorder mid-twentieth-century social studies. How can we radically reform a discipline that seeks to locate issues like Black poverty and political marginalization in the failure of Black families to integrate into a heteropatriarchal model? West encourages us to think creatively about what motivates a character like Cleo to embark on a project that seemingly dooms her entire family—and it is valuable to consider what she's gained by the novel's end even as she's lost her husband, her financial security, and the love of her sisters.

Cleo's celebration of the Jericho women marks a quest for liberation that is incommensurate with life under patriarchal and white supremacist control. At various moments in the novel, we see the anxiety Cleo experiences as she reflects on the afterlife of the sort of unhappy autonomy of her quest: "Cleo felt frightened. [Judy] belongs to me. And already I can see her will to belong to herself. I want her to be a Bostonian but I want her to be me deep down. Judy, her frightened heart cried, be me as my sisters are Mama. Love me enough to let me live forever" (141). Cleo's desire to create an autonomous life for herself, her desire to see to it that her daughter understands that they come from Black women who would rather die than be subjected to the shame inherent in enslavement, and her inability to differentiate between herself, her mother, her sisters, and her daughter speaks to some profound questions regarding the price of acquiring autonomy.

As the novel closes, readers are encouraged to believe Cleo a failure. The tone of the narrative tracks exclusively toward depicting Cleo as failed. Her world seemingly collapsing around her under poverty and the impending doom of World War I, Cleo watches her sister go to work in a "white folks' kitchen" (313). Moreover, Judy, watching what appears to be her mother's matriarchal vision fail to live up to its imagined greatness, notes, "Cleo was the boss of nothing but the young, the weak, the frightened. She ruled a pygmy kingdom" (308). Readers might be encouraged to understand Cleo's failure as twofold: her family hasn't escaped tending to the white household, and Cleo has power only over the women and children of her home, whom Judy imagines as mere "pygmies." While it is true that Cleo lacks community status and a husband with a successful business, and that she is unemployed and facing mounting bills caring for a household of similarly unemployed Black mothers and children, this does not detract from the impact of the alternative to romantic, heteronormative family-making that propels Cleo's narrative trajectory. There is another generation of Jericho women waiting. Penny, Cleo's niece, is destined or doomed, depending on how one reads the role of female autonomy within *The Living Is Easy,* because she dreams about "growing famous" and having "everything she could wish for without any old husband to give it to her" (299). Cleo believes her niece is not so smart, but Penny believes herself brilliant. And it is this tension that signals the rupture of the heteronormative model of family-making, which I would argue is West's contribution to a pre–civil rights, early Black feminist critique of nation and family.

In 1948, West offers a nonnormative family to the post-WWII reading public. She offers this in a moment when the United States is returning to the nuclear family model as part of the American Dream. From her early letters to Langston Hughes to Cleo Judson's matriarchal vision of hearth and home, West's imagination and her literary work disrupt criticisms of the domestic novel's utility for radical work. She models the possibility that radical satisfaction may result in Black women characters who are despised and socially marginalized but who are also living exactly how they imagined.

CHAPTER 3

Domestic Work

Dangerous Workers and Black Sociality

In 1956, an informant told the FBI that Alice Childress's new book, *Like One of the Family . . . Conversations from a Domestic's Life,* was being widely circulated among members of the Communist Party, both locally and nationally.[1] *Like One of the Family* collects the stories from Childress's column "Conversations from Life," which ran from 1951 to 1955 in Paul Robeson's *Freedom* newspaper. The collection is composed of vignettes; each is told through a one-sided conversation (some critics refer to the pieces as monologues). The speaker in each is protagonist Mildred Johnson, the listener her friend Marge; both of them are domestic workers. Mildred riffs on a wide range of subjects: the need for domestic workers' rights and unionization, desegregation of schooling, romantic love, Black internationalism, etc. It might seem odd that J. Edgar Hoover's FBI would care that known members of the Communist Party were reading the fictional musings of a Black female domestic worker. Perhaps an answer lies in William Maxwell's proposal that the bureau believed "black politics and black literary production in particular were powerful bedfellows."[2] The bureau may have been correct at some level because, published the same year of the Montgomery bus boycott, *Like One of the Family* works to recognize and cultivate the potential political power of Black domestic workers.

By the time this mention of *Like One of the Family* appears in Childress's file, however, the bureau had been surveilling her for about five years. Her file is relatively short compared to many of her contemporaries, notably including James Baldwin's 1,884 pages, Shirley Graham Du Bois's 1,068, and Lorraine Hansberry's 1,020. The file devoted to any given Black writer comes in at 309 pages, on average.[3] Yet, this file reveals much about Childress's activity in leftist circles and Communist-affiliated organizations between 1951 and 1958. Oddly enough, many of Childress's "covert" activities are out in plain sight, with the FBI building its file by clipping pages from the *Daily Worker,* the prominent Communist Party–affiliated newspaper. Childress can be seen planning May Day events; serving on the board of a prolabor, interracial theater group called New Playwrights, Incorporated; helping to form the short-lived, radical Black feminist organization Sojourners for Truth and Justice; and working to restore Paul Robeson's passport, among many other political and artistic activities. The FBI file documents just how enmeshed Childress was in leftist political organizing during the 1950s. Mary Helen Washington goes so far as to say that Childress was "almost certainly" a member of the Communist Party.[4] So for Hoover's bureau, Childress's creative work posed a potential threat to ideals of American nationalism because of her engagement with the Left.

Yet, the nature of Childress's work (i.e., her paid employment) would be a point of contention in the bureau during the years of her surveillance. An actress, playwright, novelist, and screenwriter, Alice Childress's career spanned over four decades. In 1941, she began acting with the American Negro Theatre (ANT), a theater group founded by Harlem theater artists who had been employed by the New Deal's Federal Theatre Project until program funding was canceled in 1939. It was while she was with ANT that Childress wrote and produced her first play, *Florence* (1949). However, in a March 1953 memorandum to the FBI director (Hoover), Childress is twice referred to as "an unemployed actress and playwright."[5] The memo writer notes that she had been acting since her "Junior High School days," but there appears to be little understanding within the file of the developmental ebb and flow of the theater and its workers.

Childress's labor and life are inscrutable to bureau investigators charged with her surveillance. Although some of the March memo's information is redacted, it is clear that her lack of a recognizable workday makes it difficult for bureau officers to track her and make direct contact. They report that she lacks a "set routine" and therefore request "discreet surveillance" to help orchestrate contact.[6] In June 1953, another memo follows up on the March request for a more expert detail:

Surveillances, spot checks and pretext inquiries to date however, have borne out the fact that the subject does not appear to have any set hours and it is therefore almost impossible to determine just when she might be expected to leave or return to her residence. On the one occasion that the subject has been seen, she was observed as she crossed the street from her house only to turn back and immediately go back into her house, thus affording the agents no time at all to approach her. Added to these difficulties is the fact that the subject's dwelling is a large apartment house which has some four separate exits.[7]

Unable to make contact, the June 1953 memo writer suggests abandoning all attempts to orchestrate a direct interview with Childress. In retrospect, the bureau officers' complaints—describing the insurmountable challenges of trying to track someone whose social and political engagements are public, numerous, and frequently listed in the *Daily Worker*—are comical.

More seriously, however, Childress's inscrutability and unreachableness signal the difficulty Black women artists and their work may pose to the state. In this way, Childress's file reveals her as enacting a mid-twentieth-century form of what Simone Browne describes as "dark sousveillance," or "tactics employed to render one's self out of sight."[8] Childress's variable schedule, her apparent changing of her mind in the middle of crossing of the street only to reenter her large apartment building, produce a form of "antisurveillance," allowing her some freedom from FBI detection.[9] Her work is, thus, a challenge to the state. The FBI memos reveal a lack of ability to value Black women's radical work as a viable use of time; additionally, the agents produce documentation of Childress's resistance to state legibility. In this chapter, I assert that Childress's creative work and her representation of the Black working class are dangerous to the state precisely because they exist outside the bounds of routine and the type of rote labor sanctioned as appropriate (and easy to surveil) for Black women.

Whereas the state was fixated on her employment status and lack of a recognizable routine, Alice Childress did the work of making

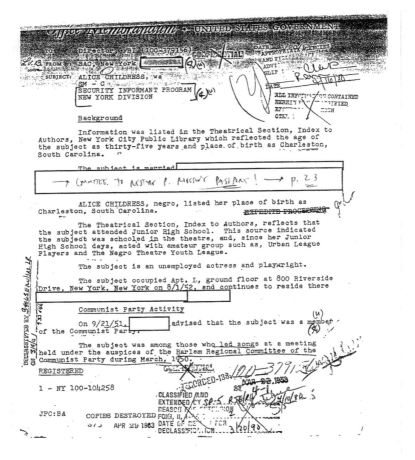

Confidential FBI memo to director (c. March 1953) describing Alice Childress as an "unemployed actress and playwright," Document #100–379156, F.B. Eyes Digital Archive, http://omeka.wustl.edu/omeka/exhibits/show/fbeyes.

the lives and experiences of Black domestic workers come to life through fiction and drama. Perhaps Childress read Claudia Jones's "An End to the Neglect of the Problems of the Negro Woman!" and heeded the call for "progressive cultural workers to write and sing of the Negro woman in her full courage and dignity."[10] Jones, the Communist Party's most prominent Black woman organizer throughout the 1940s and 1950s, held a political perspective that was "advanced well beyond the limitations of Marxism," because she was able to analyze workers' struggles through the lenses of race and gender.[11] In this way, Childress embraces what Michael Denning calls the popular front's "structure of feeling," which places her within a generation of progressive thinkers, activists, and artists committed to the ideals of worker solidarity, antiracism, antifascism, and anticolonialism, even if they were not officially members of the Communist Party.[12] Through characters such as Mama Whitney, Harriet Tubman, and Mildred Johnson, Childress rejects the mammy figure that is so frequently referenced in American culture—the Black woman as nothing more than a "faithful, obedient domestic servant" of whiteness.[13] Childress's creative labor is radical because it "sees" and seeks to capture the dignity around the lives and labors of domestic workers, while also offering them self-determination and the freedom to feel satisfied and joyful through the participation in Black social life.

Integration and Resistance in *Florence*

Produced in 1949, while she was a member of the American Negro Theatre, Childress is said to have written *Florence,* her first play, in one night, "to prove to her fellow ANT members that audiences could enjoy plays written by and starring black women."[14] This one-act play is set in a segregated train depot waiting room of a small Southern town. The stage directions set the scene: "Over the doorway stage right is a sign, COLORED. Over the doorway stage left is another sign, WHITE. Stage right are two doors . . . one marked COLORED MEN . . . the other COLORED WOMEN. Stage left two other doorways are WHITE LADIES and WHITE GENTLEMEN."[15] The signage signals both the gender and racial segregation of the depot, which serve to remind audience members of the vexed and limited access Black women had to a safe and polite travel experience. As Miriam Thaggert remarks, the built environment of the railroad depot waiting room under segregation illuminates how the intersecting identity categories of race and gender "impede the mobility of the Black woman" even before she enters the railway car.[16] It is amid these explicit markers of segregation that the drama unfolds between Mama Whitney, an older Black woman from the South, and Mrs. Carter, a white actress living in the North. Both women are on their way from

a small Southern town to New York City. Before getting into the details of the play's racial tension, however, I want to note that the play
calls for both white and Black actors. In this way, the play carries out
the work of breaking down the national color line writ small in the
theater space. While ANT's goal was to create an autonomous African American theater, centered in Harlem and capable of portraying
the full humanity of Black people, it also embarked on collaborations
with white actors and theater companies invested in racial equity.[17]
Likewise, Jonathan Shandell lists *Florence* among Childress's "interracial plays."[18] Such interracial collaborations probably attuned the
FBI to Childress's creative work, as associations between white and
Black people around ending racism were often a mark for being a
Communist and worthy of surveillance.[19]

While Childress imagines a theater capable of holding interracial actors and narratives, *Florence* turns on the misrecognitions between Black and white people. The liminal setting of a Southern train
station gives some insight into the dubiousness of a potential collaboration between the play's stand-in for white liberalism, Mrs. Carter,
and the Black characters. Thaggert writes that while the train is usually associated with "progress and ingenuity" in the United States,
"it is an evocative symbol of the contradictory progress and disap-
pointments of the post-Reconstruction era for African Americans."[20]
Moreover, within Black women's narratives, the train can be either
a site of freedom and mobility or one of potential loss and desertion. As Hazel V. Carby's work illustrates, women blues singers of
the 1920s captured the prospect of the freedom of a northbound
train when a Black woman claims "the power of movement." If that
woman is not a rambler, however, then the train whistle becomes
"a mournful signal of imminent desertion and future loneliness."[21]
Florence uses the liminal space of the railroad depot to capture an
interracial interaction on the cusp of either "freedom" or "desertion."

The play's plot reveals that Mama Whitney is awaiting a train to
New York City to bring her widowed daughter, the titular Florence,
back down South. Florence, in New York to follow her dream of
being an actress, has left her child in the care of her mother and sister (Marge) but has not earned enough as an actor to consistently
send money back to the family. Marge has little faith in Florence's
acting prospects and recounts how her sister even tried to get a job in

a department store that did not hire Black women before she moved to New York. Marge comments to her mother that Florence "must think she's white!" (8). Mama responds, "Others besides Florence been talkin' about their rights" (8). From this interaction we learn that Mama understands Florence as part of a cadre of Black Southerners pushing against the limits of segregation in order to undermine the practice and eke out fair employment. Though a minor element in the play's dialogue, the statement establishes Florence as more than an irresponsible ingenue. Instead, her work aspirations are tied to fighting discrimination and pushing for Black rights, objectives that become important for the play's finale.

The majority of the play, however, revolves around exploring the nature of bigotry among white liberals. This exploration is carried out through the interactions between Mama and Mrs. Carter, an actress from New York City. Mrs. Carter is waiting for the train after spending two days in town visiting her brother, a writer named Jeff Wiley, who is himself in town to soak up the "atmosphere" for a new book he is writing. Jeff has been stymied by the reviews of his most recently published novel, *Lost My Lonely Way,* so Mrs. Carter comes to town to help him muscle through his depression (12–13). Although Mrs. Carter is originally from Memphis, Tennessee, she performs a great distaste for the South and its racial conventions, telling Mama not to call her "ma'am" (12). Distancing herself from the South and putting on the airs of white liberalism does not, however, ameliorate Mrs. Carter's implicit racism. In detailing the plot of *Lost My Lonely Way* to Mama, Mrs. Carter reveals her prejudices. The fictional novel is about a young, light-skinned woman named Zelma, who takes her life due to the shame of being Black. Zelma jumps off a bridge to her death uttering these final words: ". . . almost! almost white . . . but I'm black! I'm a Negro!" (14). Mrs. Carter tells Mama, who is confused about the source of Zelma's dilemma, that the character must die because "she can't face it! Living in a world where she almost belongs but not quite" (14). Jeff's novel rehashes old melodramatic tropes of the tragic mulatta that Mrs. Carter finds "genius," thereby illustrating her lack of understanding of Black people (or literature, for that matter) (13). She later admits to Mama that she finds it "really difficult to understand you [Black] people," though she keeps trying, even going so far as saying that she has taken a meal with a Black person (15). Audience members should understand that all her evident liberalism and openness to racial integration only reveals her racism.

In the face of white liberal racism, Childress allows African American characters to publicly critique liberal prejudice embedded in the framework of racial segregation. While Mrs. Carter sees Zelma as "a perfect character," Mama cannot stomach the basic premise of Zelma's life and death (13). In response to the novel's principal premise—Black shame—Mama declares, "That ain't so! Not one bit it ain't!" (14). The stage directions say that Mama is carried away by conviction, not anger, and the distinction is important because it sources her passion to knowledge and experience. Likewise, stage directions indicate that Mama finds herself "on the wrong side of the railing" looking up "at the WHITE LADIES sign and slowly working her way back to the 'colored' side," feeling "completely lost" (15). So disoriented by this distortion of the Black experience, Mama finds herself breaking down the racial barrier between her and Mrs. Carter. Black self-loathing and shame do not ring true to Mama, and she tells Mrs. Carter that she knows various white-appearing Black people who live average lives. Perhaps Mama is more like Florence than we are led to believe from the earlier part of the play. Again, these minor details illustrate the subtle political work of which Childress imagines Black women capable within interpersonal interracial encounters: the resistance to what Frank B. Wilderson III might call "antagonism," the "irreconcilable struggle between entities, or positions, the resolution of which is not dialectical but entails the obliteration of one of the positions."[22] Mama resists Mrs. Carter's presumption that shame and death are inevitable outcomes of Blackness, and this places the two women within an antagonistic relationship from which no dialectical resolution is possible.

The climax and resolution of *Florence* are illustrative of racial antagonism. After the women return to more genial discussion, Mrs. Carter reveals that she is a fairly well-connected actress in New York. Mama, taking seriously Mrs. Carter's earlier assertion that she desires to help African Americans, asks the actress if she might assist Florence with her acting career: "Could you help her out some, mam? Knowing all the folks you do . . . maybe . . ." (17). Mrs. Carter agrees to assist Florence in NYC but the nature of the assistance she

offers is to arrange domestic work for Mama's daughter with a director friend of hers. Mama is initially shocked and actually angered
when she realizes what Mrs. Carter is offering; she grabs the white
woman's wrist with a bit too much force, and when she realizes what
she is doing, she advises Mrs. Carter, who has wandered over to the
"colored" side of the waiting room, that she should return to her side
to avoid breaking the law. Mama realizes the limits of alliances with
white liberals who have not done the work to divest themselves of
their racial prejudices.

What is important as the climax shifts to resolution is that Childress
turns Mama's shock and realization into action: instead of taking the
train to NYC to bring Florence home, she sends money and a note
directing her daughter to "keep trying" (21). In this way, the antagonistic relationship between Mama and Mrs. Carter is not resolved.
Rather Mama "obliterates" Mrs. Carter's position, her offer of domestic work, by turning away from integrative dialogue. In so doing,
Mama makes a monstrous turn. Stage directions again shed light:
"Mama moves around to 'white' side, stares at sign over door. She
starts to knock on WHITE LADIES door, but changes her mind. As she
turns to leave, her eye catches the railing; she approaches it gently,
touches it, turns, exits" (21). Mama's gentle approach to the color
line's material manifestation and refusal to cross and make amends
with (or even cuss out) Mrs. Carter provides the play's larger critique
of integrative politics. Childress ends her first play with a clear sense
that African American rights and opportunities will not be meted
out by well-meaning white people. *Florence* closes with the possibility that its titular character will pursue her acting dreams as a form of
resistance to racial segregation.

Like One of the Family (1956)

While domestic work is not presented as an ideal form of resistance in *Florence,* by 1951 Alice Childress would premiere, in Paul
Robeson's *Freedom* newspaper, a monthly column called "Conversations from Life," which centers one of the most outspoken fictional
domestic workers of the mid-twentieth century, Mildred Johnson.
"Conversations from Life" ran until the paper was discontinued in
1955. Childress then edited the newspaper columns and published

them as *Like One of the Family* in 1956.[23] Mary Helen Washington argues that Childress's newspaper column was in dialogic relationship with the news coverage of *Freedom* and, as such, allowed "readers to feel a personal investment" in the news of the diaspora.[24] However, without the news of *Freedom* as paratext, *Like One of the Family* offers readers a more concentrated exploration of Black domestic workers' perspectives. Throughout the book's sixty-two humorous, flippant, and poignant episodic and nonlinear conversations, Childress creates Mildred as a working-class Black woman who is alive in the world.[25] This aliveness is achieved through her engagement with her local community, national news, and the politics of the larger African diaspora. The story collection does the work of refusing what Patricia Hill Collins calls the "controlling image"—a stereotypical image that dominant culture perpetuates to justify the oppression of the marginalized—of the mammy.[26] Instead of a mammy, Childress creates a Black domestic worker with radical politics who entertains and instructs her readers in the potential fullness and satisfaction of working-class life.[27]

Many critics point to Mildred's outspokenness with her white employers as one way Childress's working-class Black readers may have derived some satisfaction from the conversations. Trudier Harris speculates that "many domestic workers who subscribed to [*Freedom*] and who found themselves in situations equally or more restrictive than Mildred's could applaud her victories."[28] There are many instances in *Like One of the Family* in which a reader might experience some distanced joy watching Mildred confront and sometimes tell off a white employer who is being racist, sexist, or more generally exploitative. In the first and titular story of the collection, readers find Mildred refusing the "compliment" of her employer telling other white people that they see Mildred as one of the family. Mildred reacts by directly addressing this familial discourse's erasure of the power inequity in the employer–employee relationship. She tells her employer:

> You think it's a compliment when you say, "We don't think
> of her as a servant . . ." but after I've worked myself into a
> sweat cleaning the bathroom and the kitchen . . . making the
> beds . . . cooking the lunch . . . washing the dishes and ironing

Carol's pinafores . . . I do not feel like no weekend house-
guest. I feel like a servant, and in the face of that I have been
meaning to ask you for a slight raise which will make me feel
much better toward everyone here and make me know my
work is appreciated. (3)

This direct address of the unequal relationship between Mildred
and her employer illustrates the capacity of the working person to
assess the conditions of their labor. Moreover, Mildred also demonstrates the importance of fair compensation for work done, not
false platitudes about family and love. Mildred's direct address of the
topic of pay could serve as a model for a domestic worker on the
verge of negotiating their own compensation.

Beyond compensation, however, Childress is also modeling the
sorts of interracial relationships that might be agreeable to working-
class Black people. In direct opposition to *Florence* or "Like One of
the Family," "If You Want to Get Along with Me" suggests that interracial interactions need not be completely antagonistic. In this
story, Mildred also has to tell an employer how she feels about being
treated "special." Unlike the titular story, the employer in "If You
Want to Get Along with Me" is more thoughtful and hears Mildred
asking for a more organic friendship, if there is one to be had (19).
Likewise, in "I Liked Workin' at that Place . . . ," Mildred describes
an employer named Mrs. L who respects Mildred and treats her
with care and thoughtfulness. This particular story is useful because
it speaks to Childress's larger leftist commitment to interracial soli-
darities that might be developed when Black domestic workers are
treated with respect by their white employers. Dignity is at the center of Mildred and Mrs. L's relationship. Mildred tells Marge that she
goes to the train station to see Mrs. L off when the employer moves
out to California, ending the conversation by saying, "I'm sorry she
moved because I really liked workin' at that place" (72). This is a far
cry from the ending of *Florence.* In both of these stories, Childress
allows Mildred to negotiate the nature of the relationship she is com-
fortable having with her white employers. This idea of the importance of choice is explored in a piece like "Ridin' the Bus," which uses
the metaphor of bus desegregation to discuss the larger significance
of Black autonomy. Mildred prefers to sit at the back of the bus and

argues that there is a difference between choosing to sit at the back of the bus and riding there because of segregation. This piece does a remarkable job of reminding folks of the sense of pleasure that comes from having a choice in the way one lives, not having to "die a little on the inside because there was nothin' to this except findin' a seat" (13). All together, these stories provide models for the power and autonomy of the Black domestic worker in negotiating their relationship to whiteness and white people.

However, I believe that more than merely offering the pleasure of watching an exploited worker confront her exploiters, *Like One of the Family* provides readers with a Black domestic worker who is both a thinker and socially connected to Black people. Because readers only hear Mildred's side of her "conversations" with her friend Marge, who remains silent to the reader, the text offers working-class Black interiority and intimacy under Jim Crow as radical work. Harris says that the text combines the literary and the African American oral traditions, allowing Mildred to have a "consciousness all her own."[29] I would extend Harris's observation by suggesting that Mildred's discussions (oral tradition) about her ideas and the events in her life and the world at large are illustrative of her deep thinking (consciousness); additionally, such thinking must be done in collaboration with a trusted friend for it to be significant. In *Like One of the Family,* then, intimacy and interiority are closely intertwined. For instance, in "Your Soul . . . Another You," we see Childress working through both Black interiority and intimacy very directly. In the piece, Mildred accuses the establishment of lacking a soul when it participates in Jim Crow (46). But more than criticizing the white establishment, Mildred reflects on Black interiority via a definition of the soul: "Your soul is an inner something that is another you and hardly anybody knows what it's really thinkin' *except* you" (45). The piece is significant because it establishes Mildred as engaged with ideas of what makes the Black individual a unique and thinking subject, while also criticizing those who are unwilling to see Black subjectivity. Likewise, in "The 'Many Others' in History," Mildred carves out a space for the unnamed heroes of Black liberation history by telling the story of her own grandmother's life; she gives flesh to the "many others" who remain nameless and unknown in Black history. In Mildred's storytelling, her grandmother becomes a hero alongside Harriet Tubman and Sojourner Truth (158). She equalizes the impact of Black women's work, allowing even the domestic work of unacclaimed Black women to serve as activism when it entails perseverance for the sake of the Black community. The story causes Marge to openly weep. In both conversations, Childress uses Mildred's thinking and storytelling to articulate a radical vision of the Black individual within a community that is dynamic in its ability to acknowledge equally the importance of Black historical figures and intimate family members.

Additionally, Mildred's conversations are written from the perspective of a domestic worker who sees herself as a radical worker, not an obedient servant. "All About My Job," for instance, details Mildred's sense of self and pride in her work. Mildred reflects:

> If I had a child, I would want that child to do something that
> paid better and had some opportunity to it, but on the other
> hand it would distress me no end to see that child get some
> arrogant attitude toward me because I do domestic work.
> Domestic workers have done an awful lot of good things in
> this country besides clean up people's houses. We've taken
> care of our brothers and fathers and husbands when the
> factory gates and office desks and pretty near everything
> else was closed to them; we've helped many a neighbor,
> doin' everything from helpin' to clothe their children to
> buryin' the dead. (36)

Although this is rather didactic, it does the work of establishing Mildred as aware of Black domestic workers' role in what Saidiya Hartman calls the "endurance of Black social life."[30] Childress employs Mildred to articulate how racism and sexism ensure that domestic work, although the most readily available employment opportunities furnished to working-class Black women at midcentury, is undervalued by the community—potentially even one's children. Without overvaluing upward mobility, the piece instructs readers in how to understand the vital social impact domestic workers have had in maintaining the well-being of the Black family and community. Her aim, then, is to foster a general acknowledgment of the dignity of domestic work.

Beyond the local, Childress taps into the international politics of the Black diaspora, indicating to readers (particularly the FBI) Mildred's radical politics. Childress often depicts Mildred attending lectures and discussions about Africa; she is invested in continuing self-education and political consciousness-raising. In the chapter titled "What Does Africa Want? Freedom!" we see Mildred at what she calls an "African meetin'" where she learns about art, culture, and politics on the continent. In particular, she learns about the early antiapartheid movement among Black South Africans. With this story, Mildred is more than a mere student; Childress depicts her as bringing her own knowledge base on Black liberation to bear on what she learns. As speakers discuss the wants and needs of Black people in Africa, Mildred becomes dissatisfied with the discussion. She tells Marge, "All of a sudden I jumped straight up and hollered, 'There ain't no mystery about that! Africans want to be free! . . . How in the devil can you sit and hear how they're starved, whipped, kept out of schools, jailed and shot down and then ask WHAT the African wants,'" (100). Mildred recounts that she "squares up" to the speakers, whom she calls "uppity," finally declaring: "FREE AFRICA!" (100–101). And it is this final outburst that places Mildred within a radical anticolonial political framework. Hoover's FBI loathed such gestures of Black internationalism among African Americans. As Kevin K. Gaines argues, "U.S. officialdom and its media auxiliaries arrogated to themselves the role of prescribing normative Negro American civic identities, seeking to delegitimize and discourage" Black international solidarity.[31] Thus, Mildred is participating in political activities and articulating the radical stance that mirrors much of what is captured in Childress's FBI file.

Ultimately, Mildred's capacity to create Black interiority and intimacy and to share an astute leftist political voice marks *Like One of the Family* as invested in the potential of domestic workers as powerful radical voices toward social change. Childress offers Mildred as a Gramscian "organic intellectual" for Black working women of the midcentury. In addition to offering direct stances on national and international racial politics and contemporary issues, Mildred also models how Black working-class women might find satisfaction, that sense of completeness and fullness in their lives, through radical political activism. For the remainder of this chapter, I will trace

Childress's engagement with radical satisfaction in two distinct ways as they emerge in Mildred's conversations: one is community organizing and Black education, and the second is socializing with Black friends.

Mildred as Community Organizer and Educator

Childress's Mildred Johnson often functions as a community organizer and educator in her conversations. This contradicts early understandings of Childress's protagonist, which often sourced her to Langston Hughes's beloved Jesse B. Semple (a.k.a. Simple) from his Simple stories.[32] Scholars attempting to repress both Hughes's and Childress's leftist leanings typically point to the characters' similarities: their socioeconomic class, humorous dispositions, and engagement with the news of the day. However, Mary Helen Washington speculates that Mildred Johnson might be modeled after Claudia Jones, as Childress and Jones traveled in many of the same circles.[33] Sourcing Mildred to Jones encourages readers to see Mildred as well-read, politically savvy, and critically minded—a fictional proxy for the "bona fide woman of the Left."[34] As a woman of the Left, then, Mildred's reflections on her working and social life are marked by radicalism in the traditional sense. One can see Mildred's radicalism in the chapter titled "Hands," in which Mildred details the significance of working people in our everyday lives: "You can take any article and trace it back like that and you'll see the power and beauty of laboring hands" (62). Besides drawing attention to the material influence and importance of members of the working class, "Hands" nimbly employs synecdoche to push unionization for all trade workers, Black domestic workers among them. Mildred tells Marge, "You can see we are all servants and got a lot in common . . . and that's why folks need unions" (63). Childress is attentive to the leftist ideal of interracial solidarity among workers, as long as that solidarity centralizes rather than marginalizes Black women workers.

In the story "In the Laundry Room," Childress further illuminates the ideal conditions and outcomes of interracial solidarity. Mildred attempts to educate a white worker about their shared status while each women does laundry. The white woman appears to take offense when Mildred touches her pile of dirty clothes, and

Mildred responds by revealing how they are both undervalued and overworked. She tells the woman, "Now when you got to plunge your hands in all them dirty clothes in order to put them in the machine . . . how come you can't see that it's a whole lot safer and makes more sense to put your hand in mine and be friends?" (109). In the case of "In the Laundry Room," interracial solidary around class and labor puts Mildred in line with that core progressive promotion of working-class solidarity. Unlike the outcome of *Florence,* Childress gestures to the possibility of interracial comradery: the white domestic worker takes Mildred's hand and affirms her desire for friendship (109). Both stories illustrate Childress's sense that leftist community organizing around labor and rights has to include domestic workers and could include interracial solidarity if white workers are able to overcome their racism.

The version of interracial friendship Childress's stories outline should not be mistaken for the toothless model of integration lacking an antiracist agenda and the possibility for Black self-determination offered by the United States. Childress is not making a plea for what Robin D. G. Kelley describes as Black people's "junior partnership in democracy."[35] Instead, Childress's Mildred is often a mouthpiece for Communist ideas and discourse around labor solidarity (often across racial lines), placing her at direct odds with the national project of integration, which does little to dismantle white racism. As Claudia Jones would argue in 1946, "Integration cannot be considered a substitute for the right of [Black] self-determination. National liberation is not synonymous with integration."[36] As Jones's critique makes apparent, the low stakes of integration are not enough for Black life. While "In the Laundry Room" could be read as a gesture toward integration, it is significant that Mildred is doing the work of educating her white counterpart; she is in the position of discursive power and knowledge production, instructing her fellow worker in the importance and benefits of antiracism on their shared plight as workers. Mildred does not condone a future in which Black people are begrudgingly given access to white people and their property; instead, Mildred's faith is in a future where Black people and white people work as equals.

Additionally, Childress more directly takes up radical issues that affiliate Mildred with the Communist Party USA's agenda and place the writer at odds with the FBI. For example, in "Story Tellin' Time," Mildred's employer implores her not to go to a Paul Robeson concert after picking up a copy of an African American newspaper Mildred has brought to work (perhaps Robeson's *Freedom*). In this piece, Mildred shares the allegorical story of Jim and his former enslaver. "Story Tellin' Time" thinly veils the nation-state as a plantation and explores the desire on the part of former enslavers to dictate the life choices of African Americans. Mildred finishes the story of Jim and tells her employer, Mrs. B, that she knows who makes trouble for her and it is not Robeson, forcing Mrs. B to leave the topic alone or be associated with a vengeful enslaver (122). "Story Tellin' Time" is an example, similar to "What Does Africa Want? Freedom!," of Childress employing Mildred to take a leftist stance regarding white censorship of Black life.

Childress's FBI file notes her engagement with groups seeking to repeal the Smith Act, which made critique of the U.S. government prosecutable and subjected the convicted to imprisonment, and with the Committee to Restore Robeson's Passport. Childress would have known that activities such as these and associations with figures like Robeson left her open to bureau surveillance. Thus, in "Story Tellin' Time," Childress reflects on and criticizes what William J. Maxwell calls the impulse toward "lit.-cop federalism," or "the desire to inject a compelling federal police presence into the print public sphere."[37] More than merely acknowledging that she knows that she is being watched by the state, Mildred's creator may be using "Story Tellin' Time" to speak back to the FBI and their surveillance. In this example of "dark sousveillance," we see Childress evoke the plantation to call attention to and criticize the long-standing surveillance of Black people. She also documents Black people's resistance to such monitoring as an act of freedom.[38] Childress appears to be presponding to FBI inspection—as Maxwell argues that many African American writers of the twentieth century did—internalizing the likelihood of the FBI "ghostreading and publicizing its implications" for her readers.[39]

In the piece "We Need a Union Too," readers see Mildred make an explicit statement in favor of labor organizing among domestic workers. The piece opens with a question: "Marge, who likes housework?" (140). Mildred's question may seem flippant, but it establishes the nature of domestic work as labor with stakes that one takes on not out of a commitment to servitude but out of economic need. This argument regarding economics is discussed in the book's titular piece, "Like One of the Family," in which Mildred criticizes her employer for misrepresenting their relationship as familial when it is a business arrangement. Mildred argues that unionization would establish set hours and pay, vacation time, and other fringe benefits for domestic workers (140). The story goes so far as to imagine a strike situation in response to domestic workers being forced to do labor beyond their contracts. "We Need a Union Too" closely mirrors Claudia Jones's argument in "An End to the Neglect of the Problems of the Negro Woman!" regarding unionization of domestic workers. Jones describes domestic workers as "exploited" and argues that the "lot of the domestic worker is one of unbearable misery" due to the undefined tasks, hours, and pay.[40] Jones implores trade unions to assist the Domestic Workers Union in organizing against their exploitation. Childress takes up Jones's call, putting narrative flesh on the bones of the issue and also putting a Black domestic worker at the center of the imagination needed to secure rights for domestic workers. As "We Need a Union Too" closes, we see Mildred and Marge sharing a laugh at the thought of an abusive employer being confronted by other white employers after she threatens to hire outside of the union while the unionized domestic workers form a picket line. Mildred's imaginative unionization narrative ends with the shaming of an exploitative employer, and it is a perfect example of how radical satisfaction works within the text.

Finally, in addition to traditional labor organizing, Childress sees the work of educating Black children as an important form of radical work. Her interest in education can be read in light of the fact that Childress taught dramatic art at the Jefferson School of Social Sciences, a Left-run (Communist-affiliated) institution in Lower Manhattan that offered classes to adults and children. Her work with the Jefferson School would find its way into her FBI file, marking her as a person of interest to the bureau. In "All about Miss Tubman," readers find Mildred and Marge entertaining nine children who live in the apartment building.[41] Part of the entertainment is sharing the biography of Harriet Tubman; however, the children have a hard time seeing Tubman as more than another fictional character. Neither Marge nor Mildred has children of her own, so the story turns on Mildred losing her temper with the kids as she outlines the history of Tubman's life. She is frustrated by the kids because they repeatedly interrupt her storytelling to question whether Tubman is a fictional character. Mildred reiterates multiple times that she is not narrating a fiction but instead giving the children the biography of a historical figure that their schoolbooks will not cover. As I argued about Ann Petry's young adult novel *Harriet Tubman: Conductor on the Underground Railroad* (1955), Childress participates in the leftist practice of providing Black history to counter U.S. educational erasure of Black liberation history. Mildred frames her story as a corrective to the American educational system: "I told you that it is not in the schoolbooks because bad folks don't want us to know about the great things our people did.... They don't want us to know 'cause if we think that we didn't do nothin' at all, we will feel inferior" (210). Her criticism of the American educational system and classroom textbooks puts Childress in line with many on the Left who saw literature (storytelling) as a means to counter exclusionary American values and encourage children to embrace critical thinking. Julia L. Mickenberg argues that mid-twentieth-century left-wing writers wrote children's books where children were "encouraged to trust their own instincts, imaginations, and critical capacities" by reading books that promoted "a sense of social justice and a communitarian ethic" and explored "histories of peoples and groups previously ignored (such as African Americans, women, and the working class)."[42] When the children ask for more stories about great Black people in history, Mildred promises them more and continues to signal that her education is in direct response to the historical devaluing of Black life and history that has characterized the segregated American education system.

More than educational desegregation, however, Mildred is arguing for curricular revision around historical representations of African American people available within the public school system. In fact, the story that follows "All about Miss Tubman" is titled "ABC's of Life and Learning," and it explores the bravery and valor of the children who were at the time desegregating American schools. Through a series of rhetorical questions, Mildred considers the psychic toll on children who have to "walk in a classroom and have no one say a kind word," be isolated all day at school, or worry about physical abuse from adults and children as they walk to and from school (214–15). Ultimately, Mildred believes desegregation is important because it appears to be the only way for Black children to escape "school buildin's that get a second place break on the money deal!" (215). Mildred even imagines a day when Black and white children will "clasp hands and walk together and get along and learn from each other and be peaceful and enjoy life" (215). The image of interracial unity seems maudlin when viewed from the reality of school segregation and resource hoarding that plagues the contemporary moment, but Mildred's commitment to progressive racial politics that disrupt racial segregation allow her to imagine a future where desegregation breeds racial unity.

The Radically Satisfying Black Social Life of Mildred

Socializing with her Black friends provides Childress's Mildred great satisfaction in *Like One of the Family*. Thus, Childress's attention to the social lives of Black domestic workers cannot be overlooked. To speak of Black social life is "to speak of this radical capacity to live—to live deeply righteous lives even in the midst of all that brings death," according to Terrion L. Williamson.[43] More specifically, I want to evoke Williamson's clarification of Black social life as "the register of black experience that is not reducible to the terror that calls it into existence but is the rich remainder, the multifaceted artifact of black communal resistance and resilience that is expressed in black idioms, cultural forms, traditions, and ways of being."[44] Black social life has the added element of combating isolation, putting Black people into conversation that builds resilience in an anti-Black world. I would argue that it is the rich remainder of communal resilience that is embedded in Childress's *Like One of the Family*. Childress's attention to forms of joy and communal bonding are central to the formal conceit of the text: in order for Mildred to tell the stories about her employers, she has to have a friend who will listen. Moreover, Mildred enters Marge's apartment at all hours of the day and is always welcome; they cause each other tears and laughter, and they are sounding boards for ideas and life experiences for each other. The openness of their friendship may seem insignificant, but the quotidian nature of the bond between these two working-class Black women decenters whiteness in profoundly important ways. Thus, to read *Like One of the Family* as a text only concerned with labor exploitation is to miss the significant network of Black social life that Childress weaves into the book. "Weekend with Pearl," "Dance with Me, Henry," "Men in Your Life," and various other stories in the collection find Mildred announcing to an inconsiderate employer that she is taking off a week for vacation, partying, entertaining out-of-town visitors, contemplating marriage, and generally attempting to live a life well beyond her lot as a domestic worker. The fullness of experience is central to understanding how the text evokes a sense of radical satisfaction: it resists the controlling image of the long-suffering and dutiful mammy figure. I would argue that Childress imagines Black social life in opposition to notions of integration that cannot imagine Black people as fully capable of joy and satisfaction outside of the white gaze.

Take, for instance, "Got to Go Someplace," where readers encounter Mildred driving outside of New York City for a country picnic with her friends. As a working-class Black woman, Mildred enjoying leisure time is a radical representation. However, during the drive, the car she is in is chased by eight cars of white people flying Confederate flags, singing "Dixie," and threatening to drive Mildred and her friends off the road. She tells Marge that she was scared of what might happen and that her friend Stella was driven to tears by the threat of attack. What is most striking about this piece is that readers must understand that Childress locates Southern-inspired racism within driving distance of New York City. And once Mildred and her friends arrive at the picnic site, the Southern-style threats of violence follow them into the women's locker room with a sign that reads "niggers not wanted" (24). Overall, the threat of racial violence is ripe within the relatively short conversation. And while Stella intends to meet violence with a handful of pepper thrown into the faces of the white antagonists, there is little recourse for Mildred and her friends in this particular context. This story is one of the few in which we see Mildred fearful in the face of white aggressors. Once

safely home in Harlem, Mildred reflects with Marge on the picnic
incident and the recent murder of two Black men killed in Yonkers
for drinking at a bar:

> Don't it give you the goose pimples when you realize that
> white people can kill us and get away with it? Just think of it!
> We are walkin' targets everywhere we go—on the subway, in
> the street, everywhere. Now I am a good woman, but if I was
> not, the law is so fixed that I can't go around killin' folks if I
> want to live myself. But white folks can kill me. And that is
> why we got to be so cautious even on a picnic. (25)

It is a clear and decisive criticism of white violence and the U.S. legal
system's unequal justice. Moreover, Childress captures the reality
that anti-Black violence is a national problem, not just a Southern
one, as the nation contemplates integration.

Yet, there is satisfaction within this conversation. Mildred and
her friends make it back to NYC safely and she promises to continue to enjoy leisure time in the face of the threat of violence. She
tells Marge, "I shall take my life into my hands and go to the beach.
After all we got to go somewhere . . . sometimes" (25). This assertion
gets at the heart of Black social life, which always exists alongside
the terror of racial violence. Mildred and her creator imagine Black
leisure as central to working-class Black life in spite of the violence
that white people often enact on Black people precisely when the
latter dare to relax. There are too many examples to enumerate regarding the violence experienced by Black people enjoying leisure,
but it should be noted that the young Emmett Till was visiting family in Mississippi when he was abducted and brutally murdered in
1955. Till is murdered the same year that *Freedom* ends its run and
right before Childress's collection of columns is published as *Like
One of the Family*. But Black social life is the hallmark of resilience
in the face of state-sanctioned Black death. Childress imagines that
domestic workers are as in need of that form of resilience as anyone,
perhaps more so.

Finally, I want to turn to an example of Black social life that
Childress writes as purely enjoyable. In "Good Reason for a Good

Time," readers are presented with the idea that Black social life must be committed to Black community health. More specifically, in this conversation we see the idea of satisfaction being bound to community and racial uplift. The piece revolves around Mildred and her friends creating a social club in which the dues are put toward education and community needs. The group enjoys drinking and hanging out at a friend's house, and in the midst of their revelry they decide that "whenever we get the notion we'll have somebody speak to us about what's going on in the world. The first speaker is goin' to tell us all about African and West Indian people." And "instead of givin' any free formal dances with our treasury money, we oughta put out some books by colored writers, and if we had enough, we could give money to organizations that was tryin' to make things better for everybody" (74). Attentive to the diasporic community, Mildred's imagined social club also provides publishing support to progressive writers seeking to uplift the Black community. Overall, this story is significant for its attention to Black social life as inseparable from the well-being and growth of the Black community. In short, we see community organizing and education dovetail with Black social life in this story, highlighting Childress's larger vision of radical politics and action as central to satisfaction for African Americans.

About two years after noting the publication of Alice Childress's *Like One of the Family* and its circulation among Communist Party members, the FBI would wind down its investigation. An FBI memo dated July 21, 1958, supplies its rationale for closing the case as follows:

> During the past five years no specific information has been received to indicate that the subject has been a CP member within the that time or has acted in a leadership capacity, in a CP front group within the past three years.
>
> Current informants, cognizant of some CP activity in the New York area, were contacted in June, 1958, and could furnish no information regarding the subject.
>
> In view of the above, it is believed that the subject's activities do not meet the criteria established by referenced SAC letter. It is, therefore, recommended that subject be deleted from the Security Index.[45]

With this letter and her apparent lack of Communist Party activity, Alice Childress's Security Index card is canceled. However, one of the last events the FBI notes for Childress is her attendance at an April 9, 1957, birthday party for Paul Robeson. The investigators note that Childress is a "writer and conducts her business from her residence."[46] Perhaps that transition from unemployed actress to self-employed writer is significant in marking her as no longer a person of interest, as she now has work recognizable to the bureau investigators. But what is more telling—to me, anyway—is that her file ends with a party. True to her beloved character Mildred, Childress would continue to mix politics with Black social life. This is the true impact of *Like One of the Family*: it imagines Black working-class life most full when it is devoted to radical satisfaction and community health.

CHAPTER 4

Line Work

Human–Nonhuman Crossings and
New Routes to Black Satisfaction

In her autobiography *Report from Part One* (1972), Gwendolyn Brooks recounts the story of her paternal grandfather's escape from slavery. Writing in the present tense, Brooks recreates the drama and action of his getaway, suggesting an ongoing rawness to the story and struggle that I want to hold fast to in this chapter. Readers join this "panthering" man, a "young slave," recently "run away from his owners," just as he wakes from a well-deserved nap taken on a spot of ground in some unnamed American woods.[1] Brooks writes that her grandfather wakes to find two snakes crawling over him. A fright, no doubt, but family lore recounts that this Black man, Brooks's ancestor, is unafraid because "a snake is not the thing that makes his blood run cold. Man is the thing that makes his blood run cold, White Man."[2] While highlighting the mortal threat white people pose to the lives of Black people, Brooks makes equally striking her grandfather's engagement with the animal world in this moment of fugitivity: after letting the snakes pass, this newly free Black man "rises and enters the world."[3] Her grandfather's fearlessness and willingness to allow the snakes to make their "itinerary" across his newly self-emancipated body grounds the bulk of this chapter's exploration of what it might mean to bind transtemporal kinship to cross-species kinship—both practices of liberation among the dispossessed. Brooks narratively grounds Black self-liberation in the life-doings of animals, and this literary act will prove productive as this final chapter unfolds.

It is telling that one can find homages to the links between Black liberation and the mundane magnificence of the nonhuman world strategically placed throughout Gwendolyn Brooks's corpus. For instance, in another section of her autobiography, Brooks asserts her belief that animals and plant life—from roaches to weeds—are also "human" because they are "things of identity and response," thus articulating a reconfiguration of the human beyond man in just one line.[4] Or perhaps we might take Brooks's poem "Pete at the Zoo," originally published in *The Bean Eaters* (1960), in which the speaker wonders at the life of the elephant after the zoo closes. "Does he hunch up, as I do, / Against the dark of night?" the poem's speaker asks, signaling an intimacy between the two figures when they are not subjected to the public's gaze.[5] Or we might look to her late-published work, *Children Coming Home* (1991), and to the poem "Abruptly," which begins, "God is a gorilla."[6] The speaker of "Abruptly," after describing God's features as simian, is told by a friend that it is an insult to call God a gorilla. The speaker instantly responds: "Gorilla is majesty. / Other gorillas / know."[7] The certainty and the power of these lines signals to the young readers of *Children Coming Home* that knowing majesty and being recognized as such are not merely qualities reserved for those most similar to (the white) Man. Line after line, Brooks clarifies her reconfiguration of the possible affiliations available to Black people, and they extend far beyond what Sylvia Wynter describes as the Western fiction of human as Man.[8] Brooks most clearly articulates her crosshatched and horizontal vision of life forces in *Report from Part One*. The human is not a category reserved for those fitting into a particular framework: a being need only have form and feeling to be human, according to Brooks.

Brooks's expansion of being is worth fleshing out because it encourages us to rethink the possible configurations of humanness—a project Brooks undertook in the middle of the last century. What is crucial in my analysis of Gwendolyn Brooks's *Maud Martha* is the novel's model for resisting the racist projections regarding supposed Black proximity to the animal that have been in circulation since the Enlightenment. These projections have been used in a derogatory fashion to exploit and disrespect both Black and animal lives. Instead, I examine how Brooks uses the domestic setting and Black womanhood to interrogate the model of Man as human through a critical engagement with the nonhuman world.

As with earlier chapters in *Monstrous Work and Radical Satisfaction,* in this chapter I am interested in how Black women's writing can counter hegemonic expectations for Black national inclusion. And like previous chapters, Brooks turns to enslavement to find new registers for Black liberation. However, this chapter pursues human–nonhuman affiliations as the modality of refusal in order to address the following question: How might affiliations with animals offer Black people new ways of imagining liberation? I use Gwendolyn Brooks's *Maud Martha* to begin answering this question because the novella is deeply domestic and centered on Black womanhood. In the text, Brooks employs a non-simile-based relationship to non-human animals in her quest for a kinship of mutual recognition capable of imagining the liberation of beings, large and small. Brooks's turn to the animal is particularly compelling, as she uses both poetry and prose to participate in and push past African American literature's more typical sentimental or metaphorical engagement with animals.[9] Instead, Brooks constructs modes of recognition that bridge the human–nonhuman animal binary, thus innovating forms of sociality capable of imagining power relations that are not based on segregation and hierarchies that do not track proximity to white people.

Worrying Lines

The affiliation between Black people and animals is a bruise. The rawness of rights, Blackness, and the animal abound in the African American literary tradition. Frederick Douglass frequently returns to the beast-like status of enslaved people in his autobiographical slave narrative, *Narrative of the Life of Frederick Douglass* (1845).[10] Toni Morrison's canonical neo-slave narrative *Beloved* (1987) takes on this topic just as directly: from Schoolteacher's listing Sethe's "animal versus human" characteristics while she is enslaved on the Sweet Home farm to Paul D's reminder to her that she walks on two legs, not four, and, thus, should not have taken Beloved's life, Morrison's novel consistently presses the tender spot of what it means to be Black and human but treated like livestock by the nation.[11] Readers of African American literature are frequently confronted by narratives that summon ontological questions of what it means to be a human denied humanity. "African slaves first bore the epistemological weight of animalization, when they were rendered as laboring beast by slave owners and political theorists legitimizing slavery," Mel Y. Chen reminds us.[12] The rise of the formerly enslaved out of bondage—having experienced enslavement as a process of objectification and animalization—entailed the mastery of and disassociation from nonhuman animals. So, while I acknowledge the deep and abiding connection between forms of intrahuman exploitation and speciesism that privileges human subjectivity over that of others, historical memory and material realities force us to consider that many Black and other *othered* subjects have unequal access to human subjectivity. Thus, it makes sense that many Black thinkers and creators might not swiftly forfeit ties to humanity.[13] But that need not foreclose an investment in the ongoing fight for liberation among all life.

That said, I want to ask us to differently imagine the relationships among Blackness, nonhuman animals, and liberation in the United States. When we carefully examine the relationship between animals and narratives of Black (un)freedom, critiques of citizenship's tether to the human begin to emerge, highlighting the failures associated with the arbitrarily exclusionary anthropocentricism of U.S. notions of social, political, and affective belonging. I pay attention to what Joshua Bennett describes as "black ecology," or the "explosion of the limits imposed by a disciplinary or otherwise aversion to thinking with the nonhuman forms of life" among African American writers.[14] I believe Brooks participates in such a Black ecology. I am especially interested in perspectives in *Maud Martha* that rest in Black narratives' capacities to unbind the supremacy of man from rights through tracing the lines between beings, human and nonhuman.

This turn to the animal in Black literary studies seems particularly urgent considering that "discourses and technologies of biopower hinge on the species divide," as Nicole Shukin writes.[15] While acknowledging the history of Black objectification and the anxious associations with nonhuman animals, segregation literature does not abandon the rights of Black subjects to the category of the human but instead offers another route, one that moves through the animal. This movement is best described not as shared embodiment but as taking the form of acknowledged and positive affiliation. It is a route that takes seriously racialized histories and affective bonds, while also seeking to disrupt the human hierarchy that undergirds white supremacy. I offer inquiries and representations of animals within

Black texts as just one route, not the only route. I do so because our lives depend on the divisions we refuse to make.

In this way, my consideration of nonhuman animals (especially noncompanion species) centers on how African American writers of the mid-twentieth century conjured the animal as a potent symbol of Black liberation. For the work of this chapter, I "worry" the color line and the human/nonhuman animal line simultaneously to bring forth innovative possibilities. Here I am riffing on Cheryl A. Wall's take on the blues practice of "worrying the line," the musical technique in which a line, phrase, or note is repeated with variation to create "emphasis, clarification, or subversion."[16] Wall uses this idea to read Black women's literature in a way that resists broken genealogies, replacing them with kinship relationships.[17] Moreover, Wall's notion of worrying the line as it relates to nonnormative models of kinship informs my own work along the color and species lines: thinking through new kinds of kinship bonds aids me in formulating new ways of seeing and of being human, of making families and history.

The sort of line-worrying that I explore in this chapter differs significantly from studies of animal similes and metaphors often evoked in analyses of African American literary representations. For instance, I have argued elsewhere that Richard Wright's *Native Son* and *Black Boy,* two of the most canonical midcentury African American literary texts, make use of animals to interrogate the Black subject's experience under racial segregation in the United States.[18] In these two works, Wright employs the symbolic labor of nonhuman animals to facilitate his representations of the violent objectification and dehumanization of Black people within segregation literature. One of Wright's tools for distilling the lasting effect of Black dehumanization by American segregation relies on the continued affiliation of Black people with the biopolitical conditions of nonhuman animals. This linkage allows Wright to mine animal life for its negative symbolic value, which can be used variously to punctuate the dehumanization of Black people. For instance, protagonist Bigger's Black/animal epiphany while on the lam for murdering a white woman comes while he is hiding out in abandoned tenements in Chicago's Black Belt: "How easy it would be for him to hide if he had the whole city in which to move about! They keep us bottled up here like wild animals, he thought."[19] Wright's

third-person narrator gets close to Bigger to acknowledge the character's realization of Black residential entrapment systemized by white
supremacy. This is achieved through a simile meant to mirror the
Black experience and the condition of domesticated animals. In both
his fiction and his nonfiction, Wright uses the animal to provide critiques of the U.S. racial hierarchy and the systemic limitation of Black
life choices: maintenance of housing segregation, pervasive violence
and its threat, and the economic deprivations that are part and parcel
of Jim Crow culture.

Wright's work is illustrative of two common metaphorical uses
of animals, both of which seek to represent Black people as injured
parties within the landscape of liberal humanism. First, there is the
white supremacist grammar used to deny Black humanity through
designations of animal-likeness. Wright's *Native Son* relies most tell-
ingly on this sort of simile. The novel is rife with white police officers,
newspapers, and court officials referring to Bigger as either an ape
or a beast. "Kill that Black ape!" a bystander demands just as Bigger
is caught by the police.[20] And the newspaper's coverage of Bigger's
inquest describes him variously as an "ape," "a beast," "an earlier miss-
ing link in the human species," and "out of place in a white man's civi-
lization."[21] The state's attorney, David Buckley, employs animalized
language to frame his legal case against Bigger, calling him a "rapa-
cious" and "treacherous" beast, a "maddened ape."[22] *Native Son* elu-
cidates the dominant culture's use of Black animalization to justify
racial segregation and forms of state violence to maintain white supremacy, couched as white safety from Black animality.

Second, there is Wright's reliance on simile and metaphor to make
Black suffering legible to a readership that either will not or cannot
imagine Black pain, suffering, and life. Such analogies function to
highlight the injustice of Black dehumanization, implicitly arguing
for Black people's essential humanity. In *Black Boy*, Wright uses the
work of animal care to point to the objectification of Black laborers under Jim Crow. At its root, Wright's animal representations reveal the necropolitics of Jim Crow for African Americans. Richard
Wright's segregation-era writing is marked not merely by the life of
animals but also by death: the killing of the Chicago kitchenette rat
in the opening pages of *Native Son*, *Black Boy*'s depiction of young
Richard's senseless lynching of a kitten, and lab animals buried under

newspapers, to name only a few examples. Wright uses animals as evidence of the injustice of Black subjection.[23] Wright imagines the precarity of Black life and death through the nonhuman animal, as Joshua Bennett notes.[24] However, such conventional employment of the animal to outline the denial of manhood and the status of a particular version of humanity to African Americans does little interrogative work on the hierarchies used to justify and bolster white supremacy. With all due respect to Wright, we need Black literature to reveal new forms of desire and affiliations that are capable of reordering systemic ways of understanding race.

Due to the historically vexed relationship between Black people and nonhuman animals within the U.S. racial imaginary (and Black people's anxieties regarding this affiliation), a formulation of the role of the animal without the assumption of rights advocacy is particularly essential. Of course, while she does not turn away from consideration of nonhuman animals, Brooks's writings do not feature easily recognized arguments for the large-scale liberation of all nonhuman animal life. Therefore, I am not analyzing with an eye toward animal advocacy in her canonical segregation-era writings. Instead, I read them as a part of "animality studies," a mode of theoretical framing that is interested in human–animal relationships but "expresses no explicit interest in advocacy for various nonhuman animals."[25] In brief, one of the lasting literary impacts of segregation literature may be how it exposes a limitation of biopolitical power over Black life, perhaps all life, by refiguring sociality in innovative ways.

While there are multiple theories and analyses spanning the posthuman, antihuman, and nonhuman, all offering critiques of Western humanism, this chapter cultivates a frame that lies at the intersection of Black studies and animal studies.[26] Specifically, I am taking up with a body of scholarship on the human sourced from forms that, as Zakiyyah Iman Jackson reminds us, run parallel and provide an alternative genealogy to the Enlightenment's rationalism and liberal humanism.[27] The work of Sylvia Wynter is particularly useful for theoretical tracings that imagine a Black being discourse as distinct from the telos offered by liberal humanism. For instance, Wynter's calling attention to the "overrepresentation" of "Man" as if it were "the human itself" allows us to work toward what Alexander G. Weheliye calls the "abolition of Man" and "the radical reconstruction and decolonization of what it means to be human."[28] Wynter's long project, one devoted to the deconstruction of the primacy of Man, inspires more general reflection on how the human subject can be constituted otherwise.

At the center of my thinking, then, is what Wynter describes as the "new genres of being human" that begin to emerge when we think differently about our affiliations with the nonhuman world.[29] Attention to these human and nonhuman affiliations within the literature is necessary to cast off the dehumanization central to the Jim Crow policies and practices that further entrenched white supremacy. As I argued in chapter 2 exploring Dorothy West's work, Black women's satisfaction is readable at the site of family configurations, and alternative family configurations allow us to both find satisfaction and explore what it means to be human—as Brooks does in *Maud Martha*.

Richard Wright imagines animals as bedfellows to Black death, destruction, and despair, but in Brooks's work, we find a different grammar of animal affiliation. Brooks's *Maud Martha* details the titular protagonist's life in segregated Chicago, using poetic language and impressionistic treatment of the protagonist's rather ordinary experiences to mark the text. Much of the scholarly attention to the text takes one of two approaches. One approach argues that there is a quiet interiority to Maud Martha's narrative, and the other approach situates deep rage within that quiet.[30] In both branches, there is an emphasis on making sense of Maud Martha's interior life.

Emphasizing Black female interiority expands the narrative resources for considering the impact of racism. Brooks moves away from traditional narratives of white supremacy and sexism typically featured in African American literature. I would add that such an emphasis also allows for a different intimacy with the nonhuman, the animal. Featuring a protagonist who is both Black and woman, much of the novel's action consists of Maud Martha's contemplation of her life while carrying out her domestic duties as a daughter, a wife, then a mother. Those duties are touched by racism, certainly, but racism is not the sole concern of Maud Martha's life. As Hortense J. Spillers notes, "The instances that disclose racist sentiment in the text are so muted and understated that they are rendered elements of the background." Instead, Maud Martha's narrative explores the "extent to which the female can articulate her own values of sanctity and ritual, of aspiration and desire, of order and beauty in a hierarchically male-centered world, limited by the idioms of the literal."[31] Akin to Spillers, Kevin Quashie argues that Maud Martha enacts an "ethics of quiet," which he describes as "the sense that the interior can inform a way of being in the world that is not consumed by publicness but that is expressive and dynamic nonetheless."[32] The ethics of quiet imagines quiet as a form of self-creation that doesn't require adherence to and participation in the protest politics that have marked the expansion of citizenship rights for marginalized citizens of the United States— African Americans, women, other communities of color, queer and trans people, disabled people, etc. Discourses on liberation have historically highlighted the public articulations of marginalized groups regarding their humanity and access to full and inalienable citizenship. The discursive, legislative, and cultural work has always been to shift the American system away from the objectification and toward the subjectification of these marginalized groups, to insist on the collective humanity of the marginalized. In this context, the public-facing political agenda of segregation literature shapes a particular version of (Black) human–nonhuman animal interactions.

What can be lost in more traditional protest fiction's investment in social realism and protest is the ability to tend genuinely to the racial work done within the domestic space. It is against many of these generic norms that Brooks pushes in crafting and narrating Maud Martha's character and circumstances, thereby allowing different forms of subjectivity to prevail. In fact, through sincere attention to Maud Martha's interiority, Brooks encourages readers to reconsider public–private dualisms that often shape the way we discuss gender politics within the social realist novel. Throughout the text, Maud Martha is aware of and measures her motivations, desires, and limitations as a human being.

In one of the few moments in the novel where Maud Martha directly and explicitly faces white supremacy, she returns the gaze of whiteness with self-regard, which is a hallmark of satisfaction for this work and an affirmation of her right to self-define her humanity. At this moment, Brooks shows readers that Maud Martha is unwilling to sublimate herself while laboring as a domestic worker in the home of a white woman, Mrs. Burns-Cooper. Even though the wages are "very good," Maud Martha refuses to be treated as a child and reprimanded by a white adult because she, too, is human. "Why, one was a human being. One wore clean nightgowns. One loved one's baby. One drank cocoa by the fire—or the gas range—come the evening, in the wintertime," Maud Martha thinks.[33] This mundane measure of a human life speaks again to Brooks's scale of analysis— Maud Martha is not waging a fight of heroic proportions against white supremacy. Rather than work within the household of another woman, a white woman, Maud Martha retreats into her own home, citing the minutiae of her life as the vital material for her subjectivity. More importantly, her subjectivity is composed of things that cannot be granted to her via legislation, access to capital, or her proximity to whiteness. Maud Martha figures her humanity otherwise, out of pleasure and Black familial love. This is satisfaction freed from Western models, which prioritize whiteness, capitalism, and the exclusion of Others.

Akin to the family lore that opens this chapter, Maud Martha's consideration of her humanity is vested in efficacy and explored through interactions with various large and small animals. Brooks's scrutiny of the most private aspects of Black labor and interiority bears on the nation's social and labor policies under Jim Crow, which rests on the maintenance of separate and unequal private and public spheres between Black and white people. Yet Black bedrooms, specifically, and Black homes, more generally, have, especially in the twentieth century, been treated sociologically. Against such mainstream sociological treatments of Black domestic abjection, for Brooks, there is social and political work done within the home that speaks to more radical ideas regarding Black humanity.

Maud Martha breaches the human/nonhuman animal divide in ways that provide both artistic and theoretical openings for recognizing a protovision of liberation seeking to bypass the integrationism afoot in the United States during the mid-twentieth century. Unlike Wright, Brooks steps away from totalizing narratives of the human that have historically been predicated on the yoked exclusion of Black people and animals. Contrary to the prevailing notion of the Western liberal human subject into which many racially gendered, sexually hyperbolized, socioeconomically marginalized persons, communities, and subjects have historically been asked to fit in order to disprove the validity of their exclusion, Brooks's work provides a

set of critical moments for reconsidering the conditions and possibilities for alternative modes of Black subject-making. We must consider the fiction of the modern liberal subject, and if we presume this
is an a priori fiction, it need not be limited to a single outcome: "the
human" as dictated by the confines of Western subject formation. If
Black interiority is a space for self-creation, it must not be reduced to
simple notions of the human that are recognizable within the rubric
of Western subject-making. Brooks's animals prefigure her humans:
the beingness of animals, for Brooks, points to an alternative method
of formulating the *human beingness* of Blackness and womanhood
under segregation.

Loving Gorillas

While not expressed in terms of animality, scholars explore Brooks's
investment in depicting the interactions between human and nonhuman animals in *Maud Martha*. These scholars are especially drawn
to the novel's seventeenth chapter, descriptively titled "Maud Martha
Spares the Mouse." The chapter revolves around the culmination
of a weeks-long cat-and-mouse game between Maud Martha and
a rodent that has been pestering her kitchenette. Readers enter the
chapter just as Maud Martha has caught the mouse. At that moment, between life and death, Maud Martha imagines for the mouse
various anthropomorphized familial concerns that compel her to
let the mouse go: "'Go home to your children,' she urged. 'To your
wife or husband.' She opened the trap. The mouse vanished" (70).
Many scholars analyze Maud Martha's decision to grant the mouse
reprieve as central to what makes her, and the text as a whole, so different from contemporaneous characters and texts. For instance,
critic Malin Lavon Walther suggests that Brooks "rewrites" the rat-
killing scene that opens *Native Son* to undo the dehumanization
Wright imagines as integral to the Black domestic space of the kitchenette. Walther goes on to say that Maud Martha opts to positively
anthropomorphize the mouse and to create a "revisionary motif
that affirms nonviolence and recenters human and aesthetic value
in nurturing relationships and traditional maternal domesticity."[34]
Likewise, Valerie Frazier is invested in reading the chapter as an allegory in which Maud Martha's anthropomorphizing of the mouse is

an opportunity for "catharsis and achievement previously denied to her."[35] Frazier sees the sparing of the mouse's life as Maud Martha's assertion of her own will and "ability to affect the external world."[36] Extending Frazier's observations, Megan K. Ahern looks with an eye toward the complexity that emerges as Maud Martha expresses compassion for the mouse's life while also taking delight in what the act of compassion means for the sanctification of her self-image.[37] Ahern notes that "Maud Martha accomplishes the same (self-)creation through defying, counteracting, the fearsomeness of the world, defining herself as an exception to, rather than an excess of, that fearsomeness."[38] At the center of these readings, especially Frazier's and Ahern's, is an unarticulated expression of Maud Martha's engagement with a type of sovereign power able to "take life or let live."[39]

It is this sense of reading animals as the site of Black sovereignty from which my work departs. I push against readings extolling Maud Martha's sovereignty as expressed by her decision to "let live" because it binds her to nonradical notions of humanist subjectivity. In a sovereign subject/nonsovereign object binary system there is little room for decentering white supremacy because sovereignty itself requires exclusion of the nonsovereign from its ranks. Black subject-making centering sovereignty has very little imaginative space to consider the humanity of those caught in systems like enslavement, segregation, mass incarceration, or intergenerational poverty, as these systems rely on the lack of access of many to affirm the sovereignty of a few. Moreover, as I will consider later in this chapter, one has to contend with moments in which Maud Martha refuses to grant life. I insist that instead of sovereignty, Brooks wants us to look elsewhere for our being; she invites us to think beyond compassion for and sovereignty over animals to moments of self-liberation and affiliation as made visible through the animal.

Brooks opens *Maud Martha*'s third chapter, entitled "Love and Gorillas," in medias res: "So the gorilla really did escape!" the narrator exclaims (7). Shifting abruptly from the topics entertained in the two preceding (and brief) chapters—one detailing Maud's likes ("candy buttons, and books, and painted music," etc.) and the second sketching a scene of small children rushing to make school's first bell—readers confront an escaped gorilla (1). The confrontation forces us to imagine how a gorilla might have escaped and to instantly begin worrying over what he is doing with his newfound freedom. Maud Martha wonders if he will eat people and, if so, if he will begin with their heads (9). Impinging upon the content of the previous two chapters, the gorilla's appearance suggests that Maud Martha's dreams (and nightmares) are just as important as the spoken desires and the daily happenings that constitute her lived experience as a Black child in segregated Chicago in the early twentieth century.[40]

Centering the gorilla, Brooks taps into a variety of racist myths regarding the humanity of Black people and their adjacency to apes and monkeys. Deeply rooted racial fantasies of Western culture have long used the ape as a means for negatively coding species permeability between Black people and nonhuman animals—namely, primates and monkeys. One need only consider the lingering effects of the racial logics at play in a founding document like Thomas Jefferson's *Notes on the State of Virginia* (1785). In *Notes,* Jefferson considers the eventual emancipation of enslaved people and argues for their subsequent quick removal from Virginia (the nation, writ small). Jefferson justifies his elimination plans by citing the subdermic differences between white and Black people and sourcing the difference to the imagined sexual preference of the "Oranoontan" (orangutan) for Black women over females of its own species to the imagined preference Black people have for white people.[41] Jefferson's Enlightenment logic persists through the centuries, fortifying the sort of racial logic used to justify the segregation of blood along imagined racial lines.

Moreover, Brooks's gorilla directly counters a gorilla that makes a brief appearance in Wright's *Native Son.* Wright's Bigger, watching *The Gay Woman* in the movie house with his friend Jack, expresses his fantasy of being invited into the white nightclub featured in the film. Jack tells Bigger that white folks in this fantasy club would run: "They'd think a gorilla broke loose from the zoo and put on a tuxedo."[42] In contrast, in "Love and Gorillas" Maud Martha imagines just what might happen if the "gorilla really did escape!" In her dream of escape, rather than rejection, Maud Martha imagines possibilities beyond the fear and self-loathing experienced by Bigger. Maud Martha's dream extends Bigger's fantasy, allowing us to imagine otherwise regarding the role of animals within the segregation narrative.

Under her care, animals provide an alternative to Black punishment and dehumanization.

Brooks taps into the Black dream state as a counterrealistic site for Black self-discovery. During the 1940s and 1950s, psychoanalysis was used as a tool for Black American intellectuals not only to discuss the interiority of Black people but to extend that interiority (which they argued had been damaged by long-term and systemic racism) into a rationale for Black Americans' rightful citizenship claims.[43] Badia Sahar Ahad notes that during the midcentury decades, psychoanalytic discourse was particularly useful for Black thinkers interested in "framing the difficult road to full and uncontested citizenship as a traumatic process [that was] intimately tied to matters of the psyche."[44] Similarly, Anne Anlin Cheng cites Kenneth and Mamie Clark's 1930s "doll tests" as a study in abjection that quantified the racial other's subject formation.[45] The Clarks' study found that Black children, when given a choice between a Black and a white doll, tended to identify the white doll as the "nice" doll and preferred to play with it. Cheng evokes Sigmund Freud's "Mourning and Melancholia" (1917) to express how psychoanalysis transforms "racial grief" into racial grievance, a more powerful position from which minoritized people can express the damage to their psyches caused by racism.[46] While "one must proceed with caution," as Hortense J. Spillers says, to avoid the naturalization of universal subjectivity implied by psychoanalysis, there is a power in using the system's tools to read the damage done to the self by those same racist systems.[47]

Brooks, writing as psychoanalysis was becoming a mainstream tool for deciphering subjectivity, develops a literary dreamscape to encourage readers to unpack possible ways of receiving the relationship among animals, dreams, racialized experiences, womanhood, subjectivity, and Blackness. In locating her protagonist within the childhood dreamscape, Brooks's narrative might seem to invite such psychoanalytic readings. For instance, Maud Martha's linking the escaped gorilla with her parents' lovemaking opens the text to a play on the primal scene that will not bode well for Maud Martha's adult sexual health. One need only remember *Maud Martha*'s "The Young Couple at Home" chapter to recall the fraught marriage bed of Maud Martha and Paul (65–68). However, because of my interest in the descriptive rather than the potential diagnostic reading, I find the uncanny a more apt approach to the gorilla and to the question of what its presence in her dream ultimately reveals about nonhuman animal and human interactions in *Maud Martha*.

To say the opening of "Love and Gorillas" is uncanny is to ac-knowledge the frightfulness of Maud Martha's dream, but it is also to allow for other relationships to take shape within this "field of the frightening."[48] This is in line with Freud, who describes the German iteration of the feeling of the "uncanny" by first parsing out the over-lapping etymological relationship between *heimlich* and *unheimlich* (*homey* and *unhomey*) in order to illuminate the familiarity inherent in some forms of fright, both novel and familiar.[49] Maud Martha's linking of the escaped gorilla to the Black home invites us to pon-der the frightening associations between Black people and animals. Brooks plays with both the familiar and the repressed in ways that require us to reexamine the relationships therein. It is the gorilla's ap-pearance amid "red draperies with white and green flowers on them, and the picture of the mother and dog loving a baby, and the dresser with blue paper flowers on it" that invites something other than the disavowal of animal affiliations (7).

The narrative's structure features a repetitious return to Maud Martha's bedroom interspersed with the gorilla's escape, encourag-ing us to refrain from assessing Maud Martha's psychic state. *Maud Martha* gestures toward the psychoanalytic, inviting its use to conjure questions of Black female subjectivity. So, while we may be inclined to consider her psyche deeply, as it has been made readable through dream analysis, what if we are only being asked to be mindful and attentive to Maud Martha's subjectness? In this fashion, attention to the juxtaposition of the heimlich (her bedroom) and the unheimlich (her dream of a gorilla's fugitivity) makes readers witnesses to Maud Martha's "emancipatory project" of "simple self-attention" and her "making [her] subjectness the object of a disciplined and potentially displaceable attentiveness," as it is made possible by psychoanalytic encounters.[50]

Maud Martha is a text deeply invested in its titular protagonist's interiority, but Maud Martha doesn't need to be analyzed, because she is bent on analyzing the significance of the world around her.

In this way, she moves away from Freudian hierarchal power relations of analyst–analyzed toward what Monique Wittig describes as a feminist and queer reading that resists a social science meant to Other her as a woman, a Black person, systemically nonnormative.[51] Or, as Quashie points out, Maud Martha's internal narrative is subject to self-articulation and self-affirmation.[52] So, early in this chapter, Brooks has Maud Martha become her own analyst: Maud Martha wakes and wonders, "But why would they not get off?" (8). This question, asked twice and separated by only fourteen words, expresses her desire to make sense of her own dreamed bus passengers' inaction in the face of the gorilla's perceived threat. Her self-inquiry suggests that we are not the only readers of Maud Martha; she cultivates her own interiority and subjectivity.

What is remarkable about Maud Martha's interfacing with the gorilla is her fearlessness and doubtlessness. In the otherwise thrifty second paragraph—eighty-two words following the single-line opening sentence announcing the gorilla's escape—we are four times reminded that Maud Martha is *awake* and twice reminded of the fact that she is *sure*. It bears noting that the narrative compulsion to repeat is another reminder of how Brooks's text signals the work of psychoanalysis, only to remove the very worries affiliated with such analysis. The dream trope is evoked not to push us below the surface but to encourage us to remain at the surface and read without fear and paranoia regarding such affiliations. In this way, Brooks is encouraging the sort of "surface reading" that grants Black interiority but refuses symptomatic analysis.[53] Maud Martha's lack of doubt speaks into a space of Black faith, which might, in the face of the frightfulness that threatens to overtake the other bus patrons, produce emotions more generative for our protagonist, for, unlike her fellow passengers, who are stunned into immobility, Maud Martha, nearly in a lucid dream, like the gorilla, escapes:

> All the people wondered if the gorilla would escape.
> Awake, she knew he had.
> She was safe, but the others—were they eaten? And if so had he begun on the heads first? And could he eat such things as buttons and watches and hair? Or would he first tear those away? (8–9)

Maud Martha's concerns at this moment are crucial in separating her from the other bus riders, but they also illuminate the implicit connection between her self-figuration and that of the gorilla. While the drama of the incident explicitly rests on the damage the gorilla will do to the other humans on the bus, it also suggests that escape from danger is possible—that the threat of a breached human/nonhuman animal divide can be escaped, if desired, and such crossings might not be as dangerous as one fears.

Returning to the bedroom and the reality of Maud Martha's escape from the threat of liberation is key for my argument, which seeks to center a liberatory poetics emerging from Black feminist segregation literature. While I am hesitant to imply that the gorilla's escape is a metaphorical stand-in for the liberation of Black people, I am intrigued by Brooks's alignment of the animal and the human, especially as it relates to the larger political explorations regarding the nature and limits of Black citizenship rights that were plaguing the United States' consciousness in the pre-*Brown* era. Unlike the U.S. military, the Red Cross, and the *Defender,* Brooks does not shy away from animal crossings in her text. The impact of these permeations is felt as the chapter moves away from the morning's dream to follow the Brown family on an evening walk. Maud Martha's mother takes the children on a "night hike":

> How she loved a "hike." Especially in the evening, for then everything was moody, odd, *deliciously threatening,* always hunched and ready to close in on you but never doing so. East of Cottage Grove you saw fewer people, and those you did see had, all of them (how *strange,* thought Maud Martha), white faces. Over there that matter of *mystery* and *hunchedness* was thicker, a hundred-fold. (9–10, emphasis added)

This passage employs the language of both delight and fear, as the Brown family walks into the "deliciously threatening" white neighborhood that lies east of Cottage Grove Avenue in segregated Chicago. Like the dream of the gorilla's escape, the walk occasions an opportunity for Maud Martha to brush with danger and remain unharmed. While structural proximity in this narrative doesn't necessarily suggest a causal relationship, proximity does provide an opportunity to consider the nature of the strangeness that Maud Martha references as she considers her movement into the white neighborhood. Maud Martha's earlier fearlessness in the face of the gorilla's escape juxtaposed with the strangeness she feels when walking in the white neighborhood points to the tension between an embrace of animality at the expense of potential racial integration.

Encounters with unknown bodies, historically dehumanized and objectified, provide alternative routes toward liberation in segregation literature. Lloyd Pratt describes similar affiliations as a form of "stranger humanism," or brief encounters with another that provide a "respite from liberal individualism" without the assumption of the other's experience.[54] The uncanny, with its ability to hold both fright and familiarity, provides a framework for understanding what is possible when Black people and nonhuman animals encounter one another as "stranger humans" in the face of hierarchies and segregation. Again, I am not suggesting a proxy relationship between Maud Martha and the escaped gorilla; rather, I seek to explore new ways to consider the potential of Black personhood.

The uncanny, with its recurrence, helps to formulate a stance of engagement that is enhanced by an allusion to Freudian analysis: encouraging the individual to face the disorder of the human condition in a way that accepts fragility and offers ways to read and reroute the self. It is this rerouting that Maud Martha encounters and perfects. Rather than merely pointing out the anxiety produced by the white gaze or dissecting the primal scene of her parents' lovemaking in "Love and Gorillas," Brooks primes for other possibilities. The gorilla's escape is significant not because of the threat it poses to the humans but because it models another option for taking and owning one's desires for freedom.

The text is smart not to completely suggest a proxy relationship between Maud Martha and the escaped gorilla; rather, the chapter highlights the ways in which the external gaze that attempts to construct the Black subject (or even the simian) out of fear might, in fact, be resisted by that subject. Rather than the so-called humanity offered by promises of racial integration, the nonhuman animal offers another avenue for being.

My Brother's Keeper

If it is the case that nonhuman animals in "Love and Gorillas" provide a young Maud Martha an opportunity to witness and consider alternative possibilities for organizing and exacting liberation, then it is with chapter twenty-eight, entitled "Brotherly Love," that we can assess the long-term effects of this early encounter. Like "Love and Gorillas," "Brotherly Love" begins with decisive action: "Maud Martha was fighting with a chicken" (151). Whatever one may say about the Black intimacy with animal life witnessed in "Love and Gorillas" or "Maud Martha Spares the Mouse," by the time we reach chapter twenty-eight, a different dialectic of animal–human interactions has developed for Maud Martha. Narratively removed from childhood, Maud Martha is now a mother, wife, and homemaker in her own domestic space, and the encounter narrated in "Brotherly Love" is no longer filtered through the dreamy eyes of girlhood. Gone in this chapter is the childhood susceptibility to the permeability between waking and dreaming life, between human and nonhuman animals.

Instead, the nation is at war, and Maud Martha is fully involved. Valerie Frazier describes the force of this chapter as stemming from "domestic epic warfare" against America's inability to "reconcile the role of women, in particular, African American women, within the public and private realms."[55] Likewise, the promise of violence seems directly in line with Mary Helen Washington's canonical assessment of *Maud Martha* as a novel in which both the protagonist and narrative form exude a "muted rage."[56] For Washington, much like Frazier, this rage is the result of repression, an expression of Maud Martha's inability as a dark-skinned Black woman in pre- and post-WWII America to publicly be perceived as capable of having a critical voice. She is mired in the period's domestic idealization, which is unable to conceive of a Black woman beyond fragments.[57] So she fights chickens, and in that fighting, we can begin to imagine a more nuanced understanding of Black liberation and animal affiliations—its potential as well as its limits.

Much like "Love and Gorillas," "Brotherly Love" engages with a kind of animal that has loaded associations for Black people. Chicken and Black people have a long history in the United States, one filled with hunger, desire, comedy, and even shame. Much of the vexation has to do with how chicken theft and consumption have been used historically as tropes and allegories aimed at the dehumanization of Black Americans via minstrelsy. In fact, by the 1800s, Black people were unjustly and absurdly associated with chicken theft in the U.S. imaginary.[58]

Black women, as Psyche A. Williams-Forson notes, have historically used chicken for purposes ranging from securing their economic freedom within an informal economy of chicken trade and preparation to providing nourishment for their own families. Many other Black women have stayed as far away from the bird as possible due to the negative racial affiliations that follow any Black woman associated with chicken.[59] So when Brooks begins her chapter by stating, "Maud Martha was fighting with a chicken," she taps into the tragicomedy of Black life with chickens in profound ways (151). The action of "Brotherly Love" unfolds in the kitchen and centers on Maud Martha's vexation at having to prepare a meal for herself and her family.

Maud Martha's muted rage, exacted in small and limited ways, provides a clear sense of narrative reflective action against the sexism and racism at work within her life, for when she wields a knife and attempts to "detach" and "hack" away at the roasting chicken, she is hacking away at more than just the chicken: she also attacks the sort of domestic duties that bespeak the idealized role of femininity of the 1940s and 1950s in the United States (151). The narrative's depiction of the household work as a standoff between Maud Martha and the chicken conspires to resist the very fragmented limitations of which Washington speaks. Moreover, it is Maud Martha's silent battle that allows readers to see her as what Kevin Quashie describes as a "quiet subject," "a subject who surrenders, a subject whose consciousness is not only shaped by struggle but also by revelry, possibility, the wildness of the inner life."[60] Similarly, Valerie Frazier suggests that in this chapter, Brooks encourages a substituting of "disenfranchised women (or every minority group), thus establishing that only when men can empathize with the plight of women will they discontinue the destruction of women's existential selves as perpetuated through the domestication of females."[61]

The silence with which Maud Martha often approaches the exte-

rior world is not merely evidence of a lack of social, financial, and political capital as a Black woman. Instead, Maud Martha's interiority
compels us to consider different sources for extrapolating meaning
from within the narrative "action" she creates, especially when this
action is devoid of other human beings. Maud Martha's engagement
with nonhuman animal life is, in this sense, always more than an allegory for promoting cultural, social, and political empathy. For all her
consideration of the value of life and their potential integration into
the fold of quotidian human life, Maud Martha ultimately eats her
"brother," and this fact has to shift any reading of "Brotherly Love."

Let's consider Maud Martha's appetite as it relates to the power
of empathy to effect change and bring about equality. I contend that
Maud Martha's chicken provides more than a racial allegory reliant
on identification with an anthropomorphized chicken. Moreover,
I believe this is more than mere rumination on the permeability
between the human and the nonhuman, between the subject and
object, that refuses to ignore the appetite that always potentially undoes the ethical will of a nation founded on exclusion, exploitation,
and colonial rule, as the United States was and is. However, merely
worrying the line between human and nonhuman, white and non-
white, man and "nonman" is not enough when appetite and desire
are involved. In this sense, Brooks reminds us that the American
hunger for Black death, to once again riff on Richard Wright, runs
deep. Brooks offers insight into the nature of desire without offering
us an easy way around it: I am not suggesting that Maud Martha is
on the verge of developing a vegan politic, but rather the text as a
whole reminds us that we must require from whiteness and white
people something more than proximity in the form of racial integration, something more than the promise of grace to let us live.

Returning to the text, Brooks prepares us to consider the work of
intimacy, which one should not assume can undo the conditions of
power and inequity. Maud Martha describes the intimacy of dressing a chicken as a "nasty, nasty mess," coding intimacy away from
simplistic amity and affection (151). Maud Martha's disgust at entering into a visceral relationship with the chicken reminds us of how
"food, flesh, and the alimentary tract are linked to reproducing systems of inequality."[62] As Walter Benjamin postulates, "All disgust is
originally disgust at touching."[63] In particular, Benjamin argues that

proximity and potential contact engenders repulsion on the part of
the human to nonhuman animals. We can see anxiety around touch
and proximity at play in Maud Martha's approach to the dinner
chicken's preparation:

> [The chicken] had been given a *bitter* slit with the bread knife
> and the bread knife had been biting in that *vomit-looking*
> interior for almost five minutes without being able to detach
> certain resolute parts from their walls. The bread knife had all
> of this to do, as *Maud Martha had no intention of putting her
> hand in there.* Another hack—another hack—STUFF! *Splat in
> her eye.* She leaped at the faucet. (151, emphasis added)

The passage highlights Maud Martha's desire to put distance between
her body (subject) and the chicken's, but anyone who has prepared a
whole chicken knows that ultimately it is an inside job. While Maud
Martha refuses to enter the chicken, attempts to keep her distance,
the chicken fights back against detachment in multiple ways: first, by
refusing to be broken, fragmented from within (a model that seems
significant to Maud Martha's own resistance to midcentury fragmen-
tation), and second, by splattering its juices into her eyes, thereby
mingling their bodily fluids. Maud Martha has been invaded with a
"splat in her eye" and, as Elspeth Probyn argues, "disgust forces upon
us a tangible sense of the closeness of others: we feel the proximities
of objects and people that we fear will invade our bodies through
our mouths."[64] In this moment the boundaries separating the human
from the nonhuman animal are permeated, inviting the disruption
of established social hierarchies and order, allowing Maud Martha to
move beyond the expression of disgust to feel something that many
read as empathy.[65]

Maud Martha may or may not be revolted by the fact that she
and the chicken are now sharing her eye, but we can see the ways
the shared membrane changes her optic, and in so changing, she is
forced into a new scopic relationship. The language of Black visual
studies is particularly useful in deciphering how Brooks is gesturing
away from traditional scopic regimes—in particular, ways of seeing
Blackness and Black womanhood that normalize the maintenance of

inequitable power relations. My thinking is influenced by Nicole R. Fleetwood's conception of "troubling" vision.[66] Fleetwood's sense of the polyvalent function of "troubling" allows us to unpack the visual field and challenge scopic regimes and "racializing structures" meant to limit ways of seeing Blackness. Additionally, the theory also challenges how Black people might even see/render the troubling of race, gender, and human–nonhuman animal relations. The adage that we eat as much with our eyes as we do with our mouths suggests sight as another site for registering the alimentary track's twins: revulsion and hunger. Moreover, if we consider eating "a racially performative act, one through which we can unveil and ideally destabilize politically limited ideas of racial embodiment," as Kyla Wazana Tompkins contends, then the shift in the way Maud Martha both sees and consumes has the potential to destabilize the hegemonic systems of consumption and racial embodiment.[67] For Maud Martha, seeing and eating are tied to an ontological notion of Black domestic womanhood, but her actual task in this chapter rests in how she might undo the limitations that seek to naturalize this socially ascribed ontology rooted in Black women's social and political inequity.

The undoing of hegemonic ontologies takes guts. And guts are exactly what Maud Martha finds herself mired in throughout "Brotherly Love." The sheer amount of entrails slopping about the chapter reinstates the visceral bonds between the human and non-human animals that I've argued Brooks seeks to highlight and shape for her unique use. This viscerality makes visible Brooks's critique of cultural, social, and political purity because it is a site of death for the Black person. Maud Martha's attention to contamination via blood, guts, and dismemberment are especially telling when placed against the narrative's World War II cultural context.

Beyond military service, African Americans played a significant role in supporting the United States during World War II. On the home front, Black farmers were enlisted to contribute to wartime food efforts; unlike the segregated Red Cross blood banks, African Americans grew food items that were fully integrated. A three-frame photo-essay entitled "Farm Family Enlists to Produce Food for the War Effort," printed in a January 1943 issue of the *Defender*, spotlights a Mr. and Mrs. Sydney A. Moore of Brandywine, Maryland, who are registering their 365-acre farm to produce pork and poultry for the U.S. Department of Agriculture's Food for Freedom campaign.[68] The Moore family was just one of the nation's 680,000 "Negro farmers" expected to produce and contribute to feeding the nation under this campaign. Such agricultural patriotism would have provided Black Americans a sense of national belonging through production sharing. In addition to food production, the *Defender* amply covered various home front food efforts among Black American consumers and shoppers: they announced the rationing schedule for sugar, meats, coffee, and other consumable goods; provided "patriotic" meal plans for how to live on two and a half pounds of meat per adult each week; featured recipes for baking desserts with little to no sugar; and advised readers on using eggs and seafood in place of more common sources of protein like beef and pork.[69] They also announced significant policy shifts, such as an administrative order by the Office of Price Administration to extend representative membership (i.e., of women, Black people, and other minorities) to ration boards nationwide.[70] Black American food patriotism was cultivated and affirmed by the Black press.

Maud Martha's narrative is a part of the same wartime food efforts that emerge in the *Defender*'s food coverage. Brooks's poetic thriftiness with language allows her to quickly gloss over the details of food rationing. Maud Martha's domestic experience is shaped by the national preoccupation with war, even on the home front: "She thought of the times before the war, when there were more chickens than people wanting to buy them, and butchers were happy to clean them, and even cut them up. . . . Now meat was jewelry and she was practically out of Red Points" (152). Meat is a metaphorical mark of domestic adornment in this passage, but the preciousness it is granted by food restriction is not the only thing to which Brooks draws readers' attention. What is striking is Maud Martha's aversion to a particular type of domestic work: dressing, which typically entails the removal of head, feet, entrails, and other internal organs from a killed animal. So reluctant to dress the chicken is Maud Martha that the narrative's limited omniscience slips readers into the character's mind as she gives herself a pep talk, urging herself to carry out the work:

People could do this! people could cut a chicken open, take
out the mess, with bare hands or a bread knife, pour water in,
as in a bag, pour water out, shake the corpse by the neck or
by legs, free the straggles of water. Could feel that insinuat-
ing slipping bone, survey that soft, that headless death. The
*faint*hearted could do it. (152)

"People" in this passage become an ungendered, unraced mass of national actors, among whom even the most fainthearted do the dirty
work that Maud Martha describes as "headless death."[71] Again, narrating the visceral becomes a modality for Brooks to draw attention
to the limits of U.S. patriotic resolve for counting and containing the
violence and death of war.

Apostrophe, Cynicism, and Anti-integration

Thus, in resisting the urge to read Brooks's "Brotherly Love" as a
straightforward allegory championing the productive possibilities of
civil rights or human rights, we are able to see *Maud Martha* as multi-
valent.[72] Within "Brotherly Love," narrative complexity is achieved
through the aesthetic trope known as apostrophe, producing nuanced, multilayered criticism of the American racial landscape on the
cusp of desegregation. Apostrophe is a poetic technique in which the
poem's speaker animates the dead, an inanimate object, an abstrac-
tion, or an animal through direct address, and Brooks employs the
technique to criticize intimacy and geographic proximity as the solution to racial inequity. Most common in lyric poetry, apostrophe in
Brooks's prose is a sort of formal genre shuttling that allows her to
perform the empathetic rhetoric that Wright's logics often rely upon
while also undercutting the possibility of empathy doing much work
in the world. Apostrophe, with its imagined ability to animate objects
and instill in them a human subjectivity, gives Maud Martha the space
to beautifully ruminate on the humanity of a cooking chicken, to ask
and consider what if humans were to see the humanity in chickens?
And if that human dignity were granted, would chickens have the
right to life or would they still be eaten? She answers the first question
through apostrophe and the second with the anticipatory smack of
her lips at the thought of eating her cooked chicken.

As a poet, Brooks was familiar with the technique of apostrophe and its power for muddying the waters of what it means to *be* versus to *be made* "human." In fact, in her analysis of one of Brooks's most enduring poems, "The Mother," Barbara Johnson contends that Brooks explicitly rewrites the male lyric tradition of apostrophe in order to ruminate on the moment a being becomes a human or, in the poem's case, when an aborted fetus is brought to life by the speaker/mother through painful reflection on its lost opportunity to develop into a human child.[73] Consider, for example, the closing stanza of the poem: "Believe me, I loved you all. / Believe me, I knew you, though faintly, and I loved, I loved you / All."[74] Beyond merely considering a woman's ethical responsibility in matters of life and death, Brooks employs apostrophe in "The Mother" to question language's ability to do the work of clarifying women's negotiation between autonomy and subjection, her own and others'. "Believe that even in my deliberateness I was not deliberate," the poem's first-person speaker alliteratively implores its "dim dears," rhetorically killing and animating simultaneously. Yet, this life work is done without expressing any clear convictions relating to the abortion decisions. What I draw from Johnson's example and the poem itself is that apostrophe is not fully able to grant life and death. For my own reading, apostrophe becomes more than a mode of marking political ambivalence: it emerges as a clear systemic critique. It is critical that we understand Brooks's use of apostrophe as her way of expressing ambivalence around anyone's ability to take or grant life.

Jonathan Culler postulates that apostrophe is "embarrassing" because the trope unnaturally draws attention to the process of the poem's speakers turning away from the reading audience and toward objects that lack animation or subjecthood in the strictly Western sense.[75] Culler notes that "when [the poems' speakers] address natural objects they formally will that these particular objects function as subjects."[76] In this sense, apostrophe mirrors the work of post-humanist theory, speculating on the potential permeability between the categories of "human" and "nonhuman," the subject and the object. Apostrophe, in such a reading, is full of potential to disrupt the hierarchies that I have otherwise been writing against in this chapter. However, Culler goes on to stipulate that this direct address animating the object has more to do with the poet's desire to transcend the limits and expectations of real action and traditional narrative form and time: "Apostrophe is a device which the poetic voice uses to establish with an object a relationship which helps to constitute him."[77] Apostrophe is a form of intervention that highlights the power of the poet to recreate the world on the page. Embarrassment, then, is in the eye of the reader, not the trope, which remains aesthetically productive rather than pejorative, according to Culler. I would tweak this by suggesting that perhaps, more than embarrassing, the poetic turn away from human to nonhuman is absurd.

Brooks seizes upon the absurdity in "Brotherly Love." However, animating the inanimate, the nonhuman, the abstract, the animal is not what creates embarrassment in Brooks's work: it is embarrassing and pretentious to pretend to animate the othered object only when one wishes to draw attention to one's power and capacity to animate. The crucial point here is that the prose novella calls attention to the limitations of liberal humanist models of inclusion as a viable mode for the Other's liberation. Brooks's evocation of the apostrophe in prose draws attention to the fiction of rights, the failure of any empathetic model that imagines a change of heart as capable of or necessary to the life, let alone the liberation, of subjects deemed to be outside the category of "human." Absurdity, not embarrassment, is central to apostrophic animation in "Brotherly Love." Understanding this frees readers to critically engage the animated chicken Maud Martha fights.

In the chapter's closing, when Maud Martha considers the chicken as "man," we can begin to see the conditional limits offered by mere boundary crossing and animation that lacks ethics. Maud Martha, while growing in her courage to dress the chicken, is struck with the following notion:

But if the chicken were a man!—cold man with no head or feet and with all the little feath—er, hairs to be pulled, and the intestines loosened and beginning to ooze out, and the gizzard yet to be grabbed and the stench beginning to rise! And yet the chicken was a sort of person, a respectable individual, with its own kind of dignity. The difference was in the knowing. What was unreal to you, you could deal with violently. If chickens were ever to be safe, people

would have to live with them, and know them, see them
loving their children, finishing the evening meal, arranging
jealousy. (153)

Maud Martha's rumination on the integration of chickens into the
social fabric reveals the way she imagines the human community.
Such a metaphorical transference is especially tantalizing given the
historical context in which the text resides: the United States on
the cusp of gains from modern civil rights legislation and the rise
of the second-wave feminist movement. The fact that she imagines
the safety of chickens achievable through residential integration—
humans witnessing their lives and recognizing that those lives are
similar and equal to their own—is hopeful social intervention.
Maud Martha's extension of the chicken having some semblance of
a recognizably human domestic experience—love, children, dinner,
jealousy—suggests that an integrative sensitivity is not only possible
but also worldview-shifting for those empowered to be hospitable.
When reflecting on her life in a 1971 interview with Ida Lewis, editor of *Essence* magazine, Gwendolyn Brooks remembers herself as
profoundly invested in integration and the promise it held for racial
equality between Black and white people in the nation: "I thought
that integration was the solution. All we had to do was keep appealing to whites to help us, and they would," Brooks recalls thinking
throughout the 1940s and 1950s.[78]

That said, well before Brooks can articulate a politically critical
stance against the promises of integration, the novella contains a seed
of doubt in Black appeals to white people: Maud Martha's smacking
lips. If we take the apostrophic animation to its end, we are faced
with the thinly veiled problem of anthropophagy the scene also im-
plies. Perhaps harkening back to antiquity's anecdote of Diogenes of
Sinope (a.k.a. Diogenes the Cynic) presenting a plucked chicken to
meet Plato's definition of "man" as "biped with no feathers," Brooks
cynically undoes the very animation that Maud Martha so humanely
imagines.[79] Maud Martha's chicken is doomed, along with any hopeful allegorical affiliations that lend to the socially and politically
marginalized a modicum of hope in a scenario that foregrounds an
integration that is given to them, placing them in debt to the giver.
There is no satisfaction for the chicken in this scenario.

In a compelling analysis of the significance of Maud Martha's lips, Ayesha K. Hardison arrives at an understanding of the gesture as an expression of her pleasure in claiming a "degree of agency in the domestic space," even in the face of frustration with the domestic sacrifices required by "compulsory acts of domesticity."[80] She reads Maud Martha smacking her lips as evidence of her self-satisfaction in publicly conforming to domestic expectations of a midcentury Black homemaker, while at the same time retaining a private self that stands as a challenge to hegemonic gender roles. Hardison's reading sees the gesture as a form of punctuation, while I would argue that the smacking is more an interrogative opening, rather than a closing—an ellipsis, not a period. Maud Martha, having dressed and prepped the chicken for baking, smacks her lips in anticipation of something more to come. In that same *Essence* interview with Lewis, Brooks calls her viewpoints on the potential of integration "ignorant" and communicates an artistic and political affiliation with the twinned Black Arts and Black Power movements of the 1960s and 1970s. That twinge of doubt was there in Maud Martha's satisfaction as early as the 1950s.

What comes next in the confrontation between Maud Martha and the chicken is the narrative's restoration of the chicken's animal status. The chicken transitions from "unsightly" food item to a "sort of person," and ends the chapter an animal on the verge of being roasted. The symbolic role of the chicken's mercurial ontology speaks to broader questions of the permeability of identity, primarily when assigned by those hierarchically situated and able to make biopolitical decisions about life and death, as in the case of chickens and Maud Martha. It is the smack of Maud Martha's lips that refuses the apostrophic animation I mentioned earlier. Yet, this lip smacking also enunciates Black (feminist) desire—and the possibility of hungers fed, of satisfaction.

The interrogative approach of that lip smack frames this as a problem of politics versus appetite. How does one see and live with the other and continue to eat? And is the granting of inclusion and attending rights to the other ever enough to undo one's appetite? Moreover, what if one hungers for hierarchies, as in the case of those deeply invested in normative models of inclusion? More than providing a remedy to the dilemmas of domesticity, the chicken in Maud

Martha's pot engenders an acknowledgment of the interconnected-ness of the national and international crises—racial desegregation and a world war. These crises remind us that anticipated alimentary pleasure is not without a price. Maud Martha's satisfaction is bound up in these questions about what the nature of equality and human-ity might be for all oppressed: not just women, people of color, and Black people, but also animals. The promise of incorporation—be it animal into human, as Maud Martha anticipates, or (more impor-tantly) Black people into the residential and thus the social and po-litical rights of full citizenship in the United States—has always had a price for the subsumed.[81] Maud Martha's lip smack signifies that she has imagined and reanimated a cooking chicken to a type of human, only to reduce this "human" back into an animal that she will enjoy eating. It is the desire to consume that offers up the critique toward which this chapter works.

Ultimately, Maud's sensitivity is outmatched by her hunger. De-sire is always the failure of the post-Enlightenment liberal promises made, and racial and species integration in the form of incorporation is still at risk of cannibalism, eating the other for one's own benefit. As bell hooks points out, "It is by eating the Other . . . that one asserts power and privilege."[82] In the context of Maud's narratology, she is the imaginative arbitrator of human possibility, able to critique the promises made by white liberalism in a moment of national and in-ternational social upheaval. Thus, there is a deep and abiding species-ism present in Brooks's treatment of the chicken.[83] I say this not to discount the innovative role of nonhuman animals in *Maud Martha* but instead to bring into clear relief that to engage in a project of Black liberation is less about equality and more about recognition of the way oppressions interact and thereby constitute one another.[84] What might we be able to imagine if we were willing to imagine our-selves differently than sovereigns over the life and death of others, human and nonhuman animals alike? How might our commitment to nonhuman life change our appetites? These are the questions that are, by far, the most difficult for any of us to answer.

In the same 1971 *Essence* interview with Ida Lewis, Brooks re-members her own home as a place of little joys: "I remember home as being a place where little joys stuck out of a pretty steady base of—not contentment; what shall I call it?—maybe comfort and open-

ness. We were at ease with each other in the house."[85] Brooks's grasp
for the language to discuss what her family was able to create in the
face of poverty and racism is central to understanding Black life in
the midst of oppressive systems. Barbara Christian states that Maud
Martha is her own "creator" and, as such, "her sense of her own integrity is rooted mostly in her own imagination," which, while it isn't
articulated in "a language (or life) of overt resistance," "does prepare
the way for such language in that [Maud Martha] sees the contradic-
tion between her real value as a Black woman and how she is valued
by those around her."[86] Christian's observation points to the role of
the nonhuman animal within Brooks's text: to provide a new route
to Black satisfaction. The subtlety of the text is one of its most significant qualities. What Brooks offers readers (via Maud Martha via
the escaped gorilla) is the realization that others need not grant one's
desires and right to life. Instead, rights may be taken, restrictive cov-
enants escaped, and not merely through assimilation or the promise
of racial integration.

"Human" is an arbitrary designation, lacking an ethical and empathetic commitment to the absolute restructuring of power and being.
Yet, worrying the lines between animal, human, race, and gender
allows Brooks's work to stand as a lingering lesson that humanism,
from liberal to post, is no easy palliative. Beyond mere thought exercise, questions of the animal asked by a midcentury Black woman
writer like Gwendolyn Brooks make room for liberation on terms
that defy integration's mandate for inclusion without change. Moreover, it is in the Black domestic space that centers Black womanhood where such deliberate liberatory work can happen. Neither the
human nor what comes after it can free us if we fail to consider the
structural limitations of what brought us here. We will all be eaten
otherwise. Gwendolyn Brooks provides new kinship forms that
might free our imaginations for thinking about liberation that does
not track us back into categories and conditions designed to contain
and limit us in the first place.

· CODA ·

The Revenant

Traditionally, discussions of literary radicalism typically, and understandably, focus on political movements related to Communism or leftist activism. I am much more intellectually, and bodily, provoked by the relationship between radicalism, Black women's work, and the possibility that satisfaction and monstrosity must be companion concepts for understanding and imagining the radical work of Black women writers in the mid-twentieth century.

While a number of the writers in this project had close ties to the Communist Party, Black women not only attended to these traditional radical politics but also carved out a space for the nonorganized radicalism that can be found in community, family formation, domestic service work, and reconfigurations of the relationships between human and nonhuman animals. In all instances, I have argued for a more elastic understanding of radicalism in the midcentury in order to make more visible the counterhegemonic work of Black women writing in a nation on the cusp of desegregation.

Attending to literary representations of Black women's various forms of radicalism, the quest for satisfaction among these midcentury writers necessarily requires the depiction of acts that the mainstream would deem monstrous, in that they refuse to adhere to normative modes of citizenship and belonging. My argument regarding monstrosity centers around an understanding of and commitment to the radicalism of narratives that depict Black women who find satisfaction in ways outside of those expected in a Jim Crow nation or offered by the promise of desegregation. The monstrous becomes the means through which these Black women writers and characters encourage readers to consider their joy and contentment on their own terms—and in their respective presents, because satisfaction, here, is temporally specific. Although Black women's satisfaction can be instigated in the past or have repercussions in the future, it is experienced in the now. Imagining the "now" for midcentury Black women writers is particularly important to *Monstrous Work and Radical Satisfaction*.

While the critical work of this project looks back to the mid-twentieth century, my emphasis on thinking about satisfaction is significant for helping to make sense of this contemporary moment. The national investment in the social disenfranchisement and "unfreedom" of Black women appears to be closer to Jim Crow than progressive racial and gender narratives would have us think. National data produced to account for Black women's experience in the United States illuminates the ongoing limitations placed on Black life well into the twenty-first century.

One in four Black women lives below the poverty line, and one in three Black children lives in poverty. Black women are 2.5 times more likely to face incarceration than white women.[1] To add injury to this list of insults, the murder rate for Black women is 2.5 times higher than that of their white women counterparts, with 92 percent of these Black women victims murdered by an intimate acquaintance.[2] This data makes numerically discernible the often-invisible life and death stakes that await many Black women in the United States. These statistics suggest that Black women cannot wait for utopic conditions to find their satisfaction. There is little to be gained from what Julius B. Fleming Jr. describes as "black patience," or "the race-based structure of temporal violence."[3] Instead, satisfaction must be found in the everyday—in the home, at work, in the imagination, or in the art one creates or encounters.

I began writing and thinking on satisfaction in the midst of a national uprising against, among many things, the murders of African Americans at the hands of police officers across the United States. Although such violence is ageless in America, the late 2010s and early 2020s were marked by the collective witnessing of the most recent upsurge of anti-Black violence perpetrated by the police (and those who believed they could assume the power of the police). In fact, a feature of twenty-first century life is that social media and the twenty-four-hour news cycle have created an echo chamber of Black death; one is nearly always subjected to another story, image, cell phone or bodycam video of a Black person being murdered for actions that often would not rise to the level of misdemeanors in the American legal system. The deaths of Trayvon Martin, Mike Brown, Freddie Gray, Sandra Bland, Breonna Taylor, George Floyd, and many more have made us witnesses to death for which there has been very little legal recourse and even less systemic change. At the writing of this coda, the U.S. Congress has still failed to make progress on passing the George Floyd Justice in Policing Act of 2021 to federally address law enforcement misconduct.[4] Couple this with the more than one million residents of the United States dead to Covid-19, and death has been unrelenting in these early decades of the twenty-first century.

As I close out this project, then, I want to reflect on the continued significance of imagining satisfaction for Black women in the United States by focusing on Amy Sherald's portrait of Breonna Taylor, painted after her death. Functioning as both eulogy and speculative art, Sherald's painting of Taylor speaks to the vexed modes of life and death that Black people, but Black women in particular, occupy in the twenty-first century. It also, however, speaks to the enduring significance of a Black artist imagining that satisfaction might be possible for Black women, even posthumously.

Breonna Taylor was a twenty-six-year-old resident of Louisville, Kentucky, who was killed by the police when they wrongfully entered her home and began shooting in March 2020. Best known for the 2018 portrait of former First Lady Michelle Obama that hangs in the Smithsonian's National Portrait Gallery, Sherald was commissioned by *Vanity Fair* to paint Taylor's portrait for their September 2020 special issue in the wake of George Floyd's murder, guest-edited by the writer Ta-Nehisi Coates.[5] Sherald has since arranged to have the work returned to the public and to Taylor's community by negotiating a plan for the painting to be shared between the Smithsonian's National Museum of African American History and Culture in Washington, D.C., and the Speed Art Museum in Louisville, Kentucky.

Sherald's portrait of Taylor is striking, and it features her recognizable grisaille technique, which uses shades of gray to create the skin tones of her Black subjects. She paints Black skin tones in monochromatic gray to leave race intact but "not make it the most salient thing" about her work.[6] In this vein, Sherald imagines Taylor in a glamorous aqua-colored satin gown against a paler aqua background, because

Amy Sherald, Breonna Taylor, *2020. Oil on linen, 137.2 × 109.2 cm / 54 × 43 inches.*
Speed Art Museum and National Museum of African American History and
Culture. Copyright Amy Sherald. Courtesy of the artist and Hauser & Wirth.
Photograph by Joseph Hyde.

of the color's similarity to Taylor's birthstone. Sherald has said that
she sought to capture Taylor as both "ethereal" and "grounded."[7] The
desire to ground the portrait in realism follows Sherald's portraiture
practice, known for featuring everyday African Americans in common poses. The ethereal aspect of her vision speaks to the conditions

of creating a posthumous portrait of Taylor. She notes that painting someone who has died is at odds with her process, which typically entails her sitting with subjects to get to know them, photographing them, and then painting from the photograph. Denied these elements of her process, Sherald met with family members and photographed a body double in an attempt to recreate Taylor's personality and proportions, respectively. Sherald's attention to detail—a gold cross necklace, an engagement ring that "Taylor would never wear"—are meant to add realism to the portrait.[8]

At its core, however, the portrait remains speculative. Breonna Taylor never received the engagement ring her boyfriend intended to give her. She had no opportunity to select or wear a beautiful aqua-colored gown like the one in the portrait. Through this exercise in speculation, Taylor is turned *revenant,* resurrected by Sherald for an imagined future she will never see. The portrait's speculative quality is heartbreaking in light of the impossibility of undoing the deadly violence of state actors. If law enforcement had not killed Breonna Taylor, she may have gone on to live a life as glamorous and full as the one to which Sherald's portrait alludes.

Yet, understood as a kind of eulogy—a genre usually reserved for marking the impact of the deceased on those who knew them best—the painting invites viewers to witness a version of Taylor's future. Sherald does the monstrous work of refusing Taylor's senseless death and, in so doing, invites us to consider the importance of living a life of satisfaction. In this case, the joy of looking beautiful and feeling beautiful in a world that often does not want to grant working-class Black women joy or beauty. While what lies on the other side of the portrait's "what if" is death, for a brief moment, Taylor as revenant compels the imagination toward possibility.

Ultimately, Sherald's portrait of Taylor signals to me the continued need for Black women to find and practice radical satisfaction. Not because it is a form of protection from violence—nor can it undo the violence of the state—but because it is the only way to ensure that the time one spends on this earth is used in the service of one's life as much as possible. The sentiment behind Sherald's portrait, imagining an ethereal Breonna Taylor as she might have been if she had been allowed to live, is powerful, almost satisfying. It is also frightening: it forces contemplation of the possibility that a Black woman's life could be cut short just as she is securing the things promised by the state for good behavior—a car, a home, a profession, a partner, and perhaps children.[9] The United States continues to devalue Black life, with Black women being some of the most devalued people in the country. Our investment in our monstrousness may be the only way to guarantee our satisfaction, however briefly.

Acknowledgments

I am fortunate to be surrounded by colleagues and friends who helped me to see my way through the dark of completing a second book project. I want to begin, however, by thanking all the writers who came before and who will come. I hope that I have captured the power of art, community, and the satisfaction that is possible when we trust in our capacity to do monstrous work.

Thank you to all of the people who have served as readers and companions to my work and me. You all have taken hours out of days to sit (in person and online), to talk, to think with me: Kimberly N. Brown, Crystal Donkor, Ayesha Hardison, Meta DuEwa Jones, Jessica Rofé, Anika Simpson, Andreá N. Williams, and Jennifer D. Williams. Thank you to Jason Young and Carol Bunch Davis for providing accountability when I have needed it most. Thank you also to my colleagues in English and American studies at Vassar College. Particular thanks to Mona Ali, Amitava Kumar, Light Carruyo, and Hiram Perez for enduring friendship.

The research for this book was supported by the American Council of Learned Societies' Frederick Burkhardt Residential Fellowships for Recently Tenured Scholars. While on this fellowship, I was lucky enough to spend a year at the University of Delaware, where I met and benefited from my English colleagues. A special thanks to P. Gabrielle Foreman, John Earnest, and Julian Yates for sharing space to write, offering sage advice, and reading drafts of my early writing during my fellowship year. This project was also supported by Harvard University's W. E. B. Du Bois Research Institute Fellowship at the Hutchins Center for African and African American Research. Thank you to Henry Louis Gates Jr. for convening the fellowship and modeling a lifelong commitment to Black literary studies, and thank you to Krishna Lewis and Abby Wolf for bringing us together virtually when the Covid-19 pandemic made meeting in person impossible. Being in the company of such talented and engaged scholars was a gift. I am especially indebted to Darius Bost, Belinda Edmondson, Martha Patterson, William Pruitt, Jesse Shipley, and Justin Steil, all of whom provided invaluable intellectual company and support.

I also want to thank LaMonda Horton-Stallings and Madhu Dubey, who read and gave invaluable feedback on a very early draft of this project through the Second Book Institute hosted by Georgetown University's Department of African American Studies. Thank you to Robert Patterson for organizing this opportunity. I am grateful to Candice M. Jenkins and Samantha Pinto for their early feedback, as well; their generosity and encouragement is the model of collegiality.

Leah Pennywark at the University of Minnesota Press believed in this work for years, always leading with a light touch and having faith that the book could be what I said it was. I am appreciative for her care and encouragement. Also thanks to Anne Carter for guiding me through the final steps of making this project into a book. Thanks to the anonymous readers who offered substantial feedback that helped sharpen my arguments. Thank you to my student research assistants, Elise Gardner and Basirah Lawal, for being available to carry out important tasks when time was not on my side. And finally, I am indebted to Ricardo Bracho and Sara Streett for helping me to hone my ideas and words.

I lost and gained family members during the writing of this book, so I do not take for granted the impact of grief or the fortifying power of love. This book would have been impossible without the work and dreams of my late grandparents, Ellen and Elmer, who taught me how to imagine satisfaction. To Kiese and Cade—who continue to teach me how to laugh, endure, and begin each day with more hope than the last—I am eternally grateful to live in this world at the same time as you both.

Notes

Preface

1. *The Gong Show* was a televised amateur talent show judged by celebrities that ran from 1976 to 1980 on the NBC network. When the amateur acts were very bad, they were "gonged" off the stage by the celebrity judges.

2. Dorothy West, *The Living Is Easy* (1948; New York: Feminist Press, 1982).

3. For more on the language of Black health and choices see Kiese Laymon, *Heavy: An American Memoir* (New York: Scribner, 2018).

4. Christina Sharpe, *In the Wake: On Blackness and Being* (Durham, N.C.: Duke University Press, 2016), 13.

Introduction

1. Zora Neale Hurston, "Court Order Can't Make Races Mix," in *Zora Neale Hurston: Folklore, Memoirs, and Other Writings,* ed. Cheryl A. Wall (New York: Library of America, 1995), 885.

2. Hurston, "Court Order Can't Make Races Mix," 884.

3. For more on the debates around Hurston's conservatism and critiques of the *Brown* decision for state-mandated desegregation, see Deborah G. Plant, *Every Tub Must Sit on Its Own Bottom* (Chicago: University of Illinois Press, 1995), 116–42; Olivia Marcucci, "Zora Neale Hurston and the *Brown* Debate: Race, Class, and the Progressive Empire," *Journal of Negro Education* 86, no. 1 (Winter 2017): 13–24; Annette Trefzer, "'Let Us All Be Kissing-Friends?': Zora Neale Hurston and Race Politics in Dixie," *Journal of American Studies* 31, no. 1 (April 1997): 69–78; Andrew Delbanco, "The Political Incorrectness of Zora Neale Hurston," *Journal of Blacks in Higher Education* 18 (Winter 1997–1998): 103–8.

4. Plant, *Every Tub Must Sit on Its Own Bottom,* 123.

5. Hurston, "Court Order Can't Make Races Mix," 885.

6. U.S. Government Accountability Office, *K-12 Education: Student Population Has Significantly Diversified, but Many Schools Remain Divided*

along Racial, Ethnic, and Economic Lines, GAO-22–104737 (June 16, 2022), https://www.gao.gov/products/GAO-22-104737.

7. Christina Sharpe, *In the Wake: On Blackness and Being* (Durham, N.C.: Duke University Press, 2016).

8. Sara Ahmed's *On Being Included: Racism and Diversity in Institutional Life* (Durham, N.C.: Duke University Press, 2012) does the work of tracing how those working on diversity and institutional inclusion are often failed by the very organizations desirous of their work.

9. Tina M. Campt, "Performing Stillness," *Qui Parle* 26, no. 1 (June 2017): 162.

10. Lawrence P. Jackson, *The Indignant Generation: A Narrative History of African American Writers and Critics, 1934–1960* (Princeton, N.J.: Princeton University Press, 2011), 3.

11. Ed Diener, Robert Emmons, Randy Larson, and Sharon Griffin, "The Satisfaction with Life Scale," *Journal of Personality Assessment* 49 (1985): 71–75.

12. Audre Lorde, "Uses of the Erotic: The Erotic as Power," in *Sister Outsider: Essays and Speeches* (Trumansburg, N.Y.: Crossing Press, 1984), 48.

13. Lorde is intent on reclaiming the erotic and pleasure in women's lives away from what she and many other second-wave feminists perceive to be the exploitation and objectification of women by pornography and the porn industry. The erotic is the opposite of the pornographic. Although I do not share that same project of erotic reclamation away from pornography, I am attuned to the source of joy as it is expressed in the language of satisfaction.

14. Jennifer C. Nash, *The Black Body in Ecstasy: Reading Race, Reading Pornography* (Durham, N.C.: Duke University Press, 2014), 2.

15. L. H. Stallings, *Funk the Erotic: Transaesthetics and Black Sexual Cultures* (Chicago: University of Illinois Press, 2015), 6.

16. Ann Petry, *The Street* (1946; New York: Houghton Mifflin Harcourt, 2020).

17. Tara T. Green, *See Me Naked: Black Women Defining Pleasure in the Interwar Era* (Ithaca, N.Y.: Rutgers University Press, 2022), 6.

18. Toni Morrison, "The Source of Self-Regard," in *The Source of Self-Regard: Selected Essays, Speeches, and Meditations* (New York: Knopf, 2019), 318–19.

19. Kevin Quashie, *Black Aliveness, or A Poetics of Being* (Durham, N.C.: Duke University Press, 2021), 7.

20. Christina Sharpe, *Monstrous Intimacies: Making Post-Slavery Subjects* (Durham, N.C.: Duke University Press, 2010).

21. Bernard W. Bell originated the term *neo-slave narrative,* defining it as "residually oral, modern narratives of escape from bondage to freedom." Bernard W. Bell, *The Afro-American Novel and Its Tradition* (Amherst: University of Massachusetts Press, 1987), 289.

22. Toni Morrison, *Playing in the Dark: Whiteness and the Literary Imagination* (Cambridge, Mass.: Harvard University Press, 1992), 36.

23. Jack Halberstam, *Skin Shows: Gothic Horror and Technology of Monsters* (Durham, N.C.: Duke University Press, 1995), 4.

24. Justin Edwards, *Gothic Passages: Racial Ambiguity and the American Gothic* (Iowa City: University of Iowa Press, 2002), xviii.

25. For more on the mutability of gothic discourses, see Edwards, *Gothic Passages,* xxii.

26. Phillis Wheatley, *Poems on Various Subjects: Religious and Moral* (London: A. Bell, 1773), 18.

27. June Jordan, "The Difficult Miracle of Black Poetry in America or Something like a Sonnet for Phillis Wheatley," in *Some of Us Did Not Die: New and Selected Essays of June Jordan* (New York: Basic Books, 2002), 178.

28. Marie Helene Huet, *Monstrous Imagination* (Cambridge, Mass.: Harvard University Press, 1993), 6.

29. Robert Hume, "Gothic versus Romantic: A Revaluation of the Gothic Novel," *PMLA* 84, no. 2 (March 1969): 288.

30. While my focus is on metaphorical monstrosity and not on embodiment exclusively, I want to acknowledge the growing scholarship in the areas of disability, fat, and trans studies. The focus on divergent and nonnormative bodies proves an important perspective for thinking through the way embodied experiences have been tied to monstrousness within literary traditions. Richard H. Godden and Asa Simon Mittman's *Monstrosity, Disability, and the Posthuman in the Medieval and Early Modern World* (Cham: Springer International Publishing AG, 2019) has been a useful collection informing my thinking around disability and monster studies as they overlap in early modern literary studies. Likewise, Sabrina Strings's *Fearing the Black Body: The Racial Origins of Fat Phobia* (New York: NYU Press, 2019) pairs the relationship between anti-Blackness and fatphobia to historicize the violence done to fat, Black bodies from the Renaissance to the present. And the inaugural issue of *TSQ: Transgender Studies Quarterly* has a short and useful entry on the keyword *Monster* by Anson Koch-Rein, which captures the dual potential (injury and resistance) of the monster in trans discourse (Anson Koch-Rein, "Monster," *TSQ: Transgender Studies Quarterly* 1, no. 1–2 [2014]: 134–35). These are growing and important fields that I cannot capture in my work but that

buttress my interest in thinking through and beyond normativity's injury for marginalized folks.

31. Hortense J. Spillers, "Mama's Baby, Papa's Maybe: An American Grammar Book," in *Black, White, and In Color: Essays on American Literature and Culture* (Chicago: University of Chicago Press, 2003), 215.

32. Spillers, "Mama's Baby, Papa's Maybe," 216.

33. Spillers, 207.

34. Spillers, 228–29.

35. Sylvia Wynter, "Unsettling the Coloniality of Being/Power/Truth /Freedom: Towards the Human, After Man, Its Overrepresentation—An Argument," *CR: The New Centennial Review* 3, no. 3 (Fall 2003): 262.

36. Kinitra D. Brooks speaks in great depth of the impact of Sycorax, the racially gendered subject, on the postmodern genre of horror. See Kinitra D. Brooks, *Searching for Sycorax: Black Woman and Horror* (New Brunswick, N.J.: Rutgers University Press, 2018).

37. Sylvia Wynter, "Beyond Miranda's Meaning: Un/silencing the 'Demonic Ground' of Caliban's 'Woman,'" in *Out of Kumbla: Caribbean Women and Literature,* ed. Carole Boyce Davies and Elaine Savory Fido (Trenton, N.J.: African World Press, 1990), 358.

38. Angela Y. Davis, "Let Us All Rise Together: Radical Perspectives on Empowerment for Afro-American Women," in *Women, Culture, and Politics* (New York: Random House, 1989), 14.

39. Marcus Garvey, "Chapter 2," in *Philosophy and Opinions of Marcus Garvey, Part 1,* ed. Amy Jacques Garvey (Paterson, N.J.: Frank Cass & Publishers, 1923), 23.

40. See, for instance, Brian Dolinar, *The Black Cultural Front: Black Writers and Artists of the Depression Generation* (Jackson: University Press of Mississippi, 2012); Bill V. Mullen, *Popular Fronts: Chicago and African-American Cultural Politics, 1935–46* (Urbana: University of Illinois Press, 1999); Barbara Foley, *Spectres of 1919: Class and Nation in the Making of the New Negro* (Champaign: University of Illinois Press, 2003); Alan M. Wald, *Exiles from a Future Time: The Forging of the Mid-Twentieth-Century Literary Left* (Chapel Hill: University of North Carolina Press, 2002); William J. Maxwell, *New Negro, Old Left: African-American Writing and Communism between the Wars* (New York: Columbia University Press, 1999); William Maxwell, *F. B. Eyes: How J. Edgar Hoover's Ghostreaders Framed African American Literature* (Princeton, N.J.: Princeton University Press, 2015); James Edward Smethurst, *The New Red Negro: The Literary Left and African American Poetry, 1930–1946* (New York: Oxford University Press, 1999);

Cheryl Higashida, *Black Internationalist Feminism: Women Writers of the Black Left, 1945–1995* (Champaign: University of Illinois Press, 2011); Mary Helen Washington, *The Other Blacklist: The African American Literary and Cultural Left of the 1950s* (New York: Columbia University Press, 2014).

41. Mullen, *Popular Fronts,* 10.

42. See Higashida, *Black Internationalist Feminism,* 32–56.

43. Angela Y. Davis, "Communist Women," in *Women, Race, and Class* (New York: Random House, 1983), 149–71.

44. Carole Boyce Davies, *Left of Karl Marx: The Political Life of Black Communist Claudia Jones* (Durham, N.C.: Duke University Press, 2007), 27.

45. Claudia Jones, "An End to the Neglect of the Problems of the Negro Woman!," in *Words of Fire: An Anthology of African-American Feminist Thought,* ed. Beverly Guy-Sheftall (New York: New Press, 1995), 109. For more on Claudia Jones see Davies, *Left of Karl Marx.*

46. Jones, "An End to the Neglect of the Problems of the Negro Woman!," 123.

47. Davies, *Left of Karl Marx,* 33.

48. Barbara Foley argues that the Communist Party and the popular front of the 1930s had a "mixed record" on gender egalitarianism that acknowledged women as members of the proletariat but not as important as men. Barbara Foley, *Radical Representations: Politics and Form in U.S. Proletarian Fiction, 1929–1941* (Durham, N.C.: Duke University Press, 1993), 240, 218.

49. The blog *Black Perspectives* devoted one of its five "Black October" forum entries to Claudia Jones. The forum commemorated the one hundredth anniversary of the Russian Bolshevik Revolution of 1917 by exploring how the revolution helped shape Black diasporic anticapitalist, anti-imperialist history. See Denise Lynn, "The Marxist Proposition, Claudia Jones, and Black Nationalism," *Black Perspectives* (blog), November 2017, https://www.aaihs.org/the-marxist-proposition-claudia-jones-and-black-nationalism/.

50. Higashida, *Black Internationalist Feminism,* 4.

51. David Scott, "The Re-enchantment of Humanism: An Interview with Sylvia Wynter," *Small Axe* 8 (September 2000): 153.

52. Erica R. Edwards, *The Other Side of Terror: Black Women and the Culture of US Empire* (New York: New York University Press, 2021), 9.

53. Simone Browne, *Dark Matters: On the Surveillance of Blackness* (Durham, N.C.: Duke University Press, 2015), 22–23.

1. Ugly Work

1. Courtney Vinopal, "'The Street' Is Our May Book Club Pick," PBS NewsHour, April 29, 2020, https://www.pbs.org/newshour/arts/the -street-is-our-may-book-club-pick.

2. Michael Eric Dyson, "Where Do We Go after Ferguson?," *New York Times,* November 29, 2014, https://www.nytimes.com/2014/11/30 /opinion/sunday/where-do-we-go-after-ferguson.html. In this piece, Dyson notes the scene in which the police murder a Black man and leave his body on the street for hours. Lutie sees the body and scene and reflects on what would make a man's life worth so little to the police.

3. Tayari Jones, "In Praise of Ann Petry," *New York Times,* November 10, 2018, https://www.nytimes.com/2018/11/10/books/review/in-praise -of-ann-petry.html. While #MeToo gained national and international traction in October 2017 on the heels of a series of Hollywood sexual assault scandals, activist Tarana Burke takes credit for introducing the phrase as early as 2006. For an early journalistic attribution of the "me too" phrasing to Burke, see Abby Ohlheiser, "The Woman behind 'Me Too' Knew the Power of the Phrase When She Created It—10 Years Ago," *Washington Post,* October 19, 2017, https://www.washingtonpost.com/news/the -intersect/wp/2017/10/19/the-woman-behind-me-too-knew-the-power -of-the-phrase-when-she-created-it-10-years-ago.

4. It should be noted that some historians have argued that Tituba was of mixed Indigenous and African descent. Petry writes her as Black.

5. For more on the exploration of Petry's critique of masculinity and gender, see chapters 2 and 3 of Keith Clark, *The Radical Fiction of Ann Petry* (Baton Rouge: Louisiana State University Press, 2013).

6. *Oxford English Dictionary,* s.v. "ugly (*adj., adv.,* & *n.*), Etymology," accessed March 2024, https://doi.org/10.1093/OED/5948338727.

7. W. E. B. Du Bois, "A Negro Student at Harvard at the End of the 19th Century," *Massachusetts Review* 1, no. 2 (Spring 1960): 443.

8. Ann Petry, "Ann Petry," in *Contemporary Authors: Autobiography Series,* vol. 6, ed. Adele Sarkissian (Detroit: Gale Research Company, 1988), 257.

9. Petry, "Ann Petry," 254.

10. Wilson stipulates in the preface of *Our Nig* that she writes the novel appealing to her "colored brethren" for their patronage. See Harriet E. Wilson, preface to *Our Nig; Or, Sketches from the Life of a Free Black,* ed. Gabrielle Foreman and Reginald H. Pitts (New York: Penguin Books, 2009).

11. Petry, "Ann Petry," 253.

12. Robert A. Bone, *The Negro Novel in America* (New Haven, Conn.: Yale University Press, 1965), 180.

13. Bone, *Negro Novel in America*, 180. Bone seems to deride *The Street* to favor Petry's second novel, *A Country Place* (1947), which features an all-white cast of characters and focuses on small-town life.

14. Bernard W. Bell, *The Afro-American Novel and Its Tradition* (Amherst: University of Massachusetts Press, 1987), 183.

15. Mary Helen Washington, *Invented Lives: Narratives of Black Women 1860–1960* (New York: Anchor Press, 1987), 298.

16. Farah Jasmine Griffin, *Harlem Nocturne: Women Artists and Progressive Politics during World War II* (New York: Basic Civitas, 2013), 108.

17. For more on Black New England's literary tradition, see Edward Clark, *Black Writers in New England: A Bibliography, with Biographical Notes, of Books by and about Afro-American Writers Associated with New England in the Collection of Afro-American Literature, Suffolk University, Museum of Afro-American History, Boston African American National Historic Site* (Boston: U.S. Department of the Interior, National Park Service, 1985).

18. Ann Petry, "The Witness," in *Miss Muriel and Other Stories* (1971; Evanston, Ill.: Northwestern University Press, 2017), 229.

19. Ann Petry, "The Novel as Social Criticism," in *The Writer's Book,* ed. Helen Hull (New York: Harpers, 1950), 32.

20. On the topic of Petry's radicalism, Keith Clark is among the contemporary scholars urging for a fuller treatment of Petry's corpus. In his manuscript dedicated to Petry, Clark mines her work for a "radical aesthetic agenda" and encourages future scholars to "showcase her radical departures from standard discursive praxes in the 1940s and 1950s." See Clark, *Radical Fiction of Ann Petry,* 6–7. Likewise, the "radical aesthetic agenda" of Petry's writing, according to Clark, centers around genre, representation, and form; Clark presents Petry's manipulation of gothic tropes, her antiessentialist gender representations, and her attention to musical traditions as evidence of her innovation. Alex Lubin's edited volume *Revising the Blueprint: Ann Petry and the Literary Left* (Jackson: University of Mississippi Press, 2007) also offers a variety of essays that expand the critical scope of Petry's work beyond the tropes of social realism and locate Petry's work as a bridge between the popular front and Black Arts movements.

21. See Gretchen Henderson, *Ugliness: A Cultural History* (London: Reaktion Books, 2015); for approaches to beauty and ugliness within Africa and its diasporas, see Sarah Nuttall, ed., *Beautiful/Ugly: African and Diaspora Aesthetics* (Durham, N.C.: Duke University Press, 2006).

22. Tressie McMillan Cottom, "In the Name of Beauty," in *Thick: And Other Essays* (New York: New Press, 2019), 44.

23. Cottom, "In the Name of Beauty," 59.

24. Theodor W. Adorno, *Aesthetic Theory,* ed. Gretel Adorno and Rolf Tiedemann (New York: Continuum, 1999), 46.

25. Lori Merish, *Archives of Labor: Working-Class Women and Literary Culture in the Antebellum United States* (Durham, N.C.: Duke University Press, 2017), 8.

26. Cottom, "In the Name of Beauty," 68.

27. For more on Lutie's body and sexualization, see Rosemarie Garland Thomson, "Ann Petry's Mrs. Hedges and the Evil, One-Eyed Girl: A Feminist Exploration of the Physically Disabled Female Subject," *Women's Studies* 24, no. 6 (1995): 599–614; Theodore Gross, "Ann Petry: The Novelist as Social Critic," in *Black Fiction: New Studies in the Afro-American Novel since 1945,* ed. Robert Lee (New York: Vision Press, 1980); Gayle Wurst, "Ben Franklin in Harlem: The Drama of Deferral in Ann Petry's *The Street,*" in *Deferring a Dream: Literary Sub-versions of the American Columbiad,* ed. Gert Buelens and Ernst Rudin (Basel, Switzerland: Birkhäuser, 1994), 1–23.

28. Lawrence P. Jackson, *The Indignant Generation: A Narrative History of African American Writers and Critics, 1934–1960* (Princeton, N.J.: Princeton University Press, 2011), 230, 232.

29. Ann Petry, *The Street* (1946; New York: Houghton Mifflin Harcourt, 2020), 43. All future references will appear in-text as parenthetical citation.

30. Keith Clark, "A Distaff Dream Deferred? Ann Petry and the Art of Subversion," *African American Review* 26, no. 3 (Fall 1992): 503.

31. For early work on Lutie's commitment to the American Dream by way of Petry's allusions to Benjamin Franklin's autobiography, see Gross, "Ann Petry"; Wurst, "Ben Franklin in Harlem."

32. Candice M. Jenkins, *Private Lives, Public Relations: Regulating Black Intimacy* (Minneapolis: University of Minnesota Press, 2007), 14.

33. For more on Jane Crow and Black women's literature, see Ayesha K. Hardison, *Writing through Jane Crow: Race and Gender Politics in African American Literature* (Charlottesville: University of Virginia Press, 2014).

34. Hazel V. Carby, *Reconstructing Womanhood: The Emergence of the Afro-American Woman Novelist* (New York: Oxford University Press, 1987), 26–27.

35. Cottom, "In the Name of Beauty," 65.

36. Trudier Harris, *From Mammies to Militants: Domestics in Black American Literature* (Philadelphia: Temple University Press, 1982), 96.

37. Yetta Howard, *Ugly Differences: Queer Female Sexuality in the Underground* (Chicago: University of Illinois Press, 2018), 3.

38. Marjorie Pryse, "'Pattern against the Sky': Deism and Motherhood in Ann Petry's *The Street*," in *Conjuring: Black Women, Fiction, and Literary Tradition*, ed. Marjorie Pryse and Hortense J. Spillers (Bloomington: Indiana University Press, 1985), 116–31.

39. Evie Shockley, "Buried Alive: Gothic Homelessness, Black Women's Sexuality, and (Living) Death in Ann Petry's *The Street*," *African American Review* 40, no. 3 (Fall 2006): 451.

40. Carol E. Henderson, *Scarring the Black Body: Race and Representation in African American Literature* (Columbia: University of Missouri Press, 2002), 132.

41. Lindon Barrett, *Blackness and Value: Seeing Double* (New York: Cambridge University Press, 1999), 106.

42. Saidiya Hartman, *Wayward Lives, Beautiful Experiments: Intimate Histories of Social Upheaval* (New York: W. W. Norton, 2019), 24.

43. LaShawn Harris, *Sex Workers, Psychics, and Numbers Runners: Black Women in New York City's Underground Economy* (Urbana: University of Illinois Press, 2016), 7.

44. Bill V. Mullen, "Object Lessons," in *Revising the Blueprint: Ann Petry and the Literary Left* (Jackson: University of Mississippi Press, 2007), 46.

45. Cathy J. Cohen, "Deviance as Resistance: A New Research Agenda for the Study of Black Politics," *Du Bois Review* 1, no. 1 (March 2004): 32.

46. Hartman, *Wayward Lives, Beautiful Experiments*, 223.

47. Although it comes a bit after Petry's early work, I'm thinking of a text like Amiri Baraka and Fundi's *In Our Terribleness: Some Elements and Meaning in Black Style* (New York: Bobbs-Merrill Company, 1970).

48. Cynthia M. Blair, *I've Got to Make My Livin': Black Women's Sex Work in Turn-of-the-Century Chicago* (Chicago: University of Chicago Press, 2010), 23.

49. See Katharine Capshaw and Anna Mae Duane, eds., *Who Writes for Black Children? African American Children's Literature before 1900* (Minneapolis: University of Minnesota Press, 2017).

50. Katharine Capshaw and Anna Mae Duane, "Introduction: The Radical Work of Reading Black Children in the Era of Slavery and Reconstruction," in Capshaw and Duane, *Who Writes for Black Children?*, xi.

51. Katharine Capshaw, "Children's Literature of the Harlem Renaissance," in *A History of the Harlem Renaissance*, ed. Rachel Farebrother and Miriam Thaggert (Cambridge: Cambridge University Press, 2021), 175.

52. Julia Mickenberg, "Civil Rights, History, and the Left: Inventing the Juvenile Black Biography," *MELUS* 27, no. 2 (Summer 2002): 65.

53. Mickenberg, "Civil Rights, History, and the Left," 67.

54. Mickenberg, 68.

55. From puzzles and cartoons to Hollywood films and public memorials, Tubman's reach in the popular imagination is solidified in ways that make her a household name for many living in the United States. For more on Tubman's role in the public imaginary, see Janell Hobson, "Between History and Fantasy: Harriet Tubman in the Artistic and Popular Imaginary," *Meridians: Feminism, Race, Transnationalism* 12, no. 2 (September 2014): 50–77. Likewise, Katharine Capshaw notes that Tubman featured in many of W. E. B. Du Bois's and Jessie Fauset's *Brownies' Book* series. See Capshaw, "Children's Literature of the Harlem Renaissance."

56. "'Go to Freedom': Harriet Tubman," *Freedom*, November 1950, 5.

57. Sarah H. Bradford, *Scenes in the Life of Harriet Tubman* (Auburn, N.Y.: Moses Printer, 1869), 3.

58. Bradford, *Scenes in the Life of Harriet Tubman*, 8.

59. Bradford claims that the letters in the body of the text are included because she is pressed for time and unable to craft a more seamless narrative. Bradford, 47.

60. Bradford, 8.

61. Bradford, 48.

62. Fred Moten, "An Interview with Fred Moten, Part 1," interview by Adam Fitzgerald, Literary Hub, August 5, 2015, https://lithub.com /an-interview-with-fred-moten-pt-i/.

63. Ann Petry, *Harriet Tubman: Conductor on the Underground Railroad* (1955; New York: Amistad, 2018), 9. Future citations will appear parenthetically.

64. Tiffany Lethabo King, *The Black Shoals: Offshore Formations of Black and Native Studies* (Durham, N.C.: Duke University Press, 2019), 129.

65. Ann Petry, *Tituba of Salem Village* (New York: Thomas Y. Crowell Company, 1964), 4–5. Future citations will appear parenthetically.

66. I'm riffing on Hortense J. Spillers's definition of *captive flesh* and atomizing within the context of slavery: "This profitable 'atomizing' of the captive body provides another angle on the divided flesh: we lose any hint or suggestion of a dimension of ethics, of relatedness between human personality and its anatomical features, between one human personality and another, between human personality and cultural institutions." See Hortense J. Spillers, "Mama's Baby, Papa's Maybe: An American Grammar Book," *Diacritics* 17, no. 2 (Summer 1987): 68.

2. Home Work

1. Dorothy West, Letter to Langston Hughes, May 26, 1932, Langston Hughes Collection, JWJ MSS 28 (f. 3094), Yale Collection of American Literature, Beinecke Rare Book and Manuscript Library, Yale University Library.

2. See Joy Gleason Carew, "Langston Hughes and the Black and White Film Group," in *Blacks, Reds, and Russians: Sojourners in Search of Soviet Promise* (New Brunswick, N.J.: Rutgers University Press, 2008), 115–39.

3. Arnold Rampersad, *The Life of Langston Hughes,* vol. 1, *1920–1941* (New York: Oxford University Press, 1986), 268.

4. Verner Mitchell and Cynthia Davis, *Literary Sisters: Dorothy West and Her Circle, a Biography of the Harlem Renaissance* (New Brunswick, N.J.: Rutgers University Press, 2012), 143.

5. Mary Christopher, "Russian Correspondence," *Challenge* 1, no. 2 (September 1934), Dorothy West Papers, MC 676 Vt-17 (box 9, f. 23), Schlesinger Library on the History of Women in America, Radcliffe Institute for Advanced Study, Harvard University.

6. Claudia Tate, *Domestic Allegories of Political Desire: The Black Heroine's Text at the Turn of the Century* (New York: Oxford University Press, 1992), 9.

7. Tate, *Domestic Allegories of Political Desire,* 11.

8. Saidiya Hartman, "The Belly of the World: A Note on Black Women's Labors," *Souls* 18, vol. 1 (January–March 2016): 166.

9. Hartman, "Belly of the World," 171.

10. Langston Hughes, "A Song to a Negro Wash-Woman," in *The Collected Poems of Langston Hughes,* ed. Arnold Rampersad (New York: Knopf, 1994), 41–42.

11. Hartman, "Belly of the World," 171.

12. E. Franklin Frazier, *The Negro Family in the United States* (Chicago: University of Chicago Press, 1939), 146–59.

13. Frazier, *Negro Family in the United States,* 163–81.

14. U.S. Department of Labor, Office of Policy Planning and Research, *The Negro Family: The Case for National Action* (Westport, Conn.: Greenwood Press, 1965), 30, 36.

15. Cherene M. Sherrard-Johnson, *Dorothy West's Paradise: A Biography of Class and Color* (New Brunswick, N.J.: Rutgers University Press, 2012), 126–28.

16. Dorothy West, "Dear Reader," *Challenge* 1, no. 1 (March 1934): 39, Dorothy West Papers, MC 676 Vt-17 (box 9, f. 23), Schlesinger Library on

the History of Women in America, Radcliffe Institute for Advanced Study, Harvard University.

17. West, "Dear Reader," (March 1934), 39.

18. For Black organizing and Communism in the American South, see Robin D. G. Kelley, *Hammer and Hoe: Alabama Communists during the Great Depression,* 25th anniversary ed. (Chapel Hill: University of North Carolina Press, 2015).

19. Dorothy West, "Dear Reader," *Challenge* 1, no. 2 (September 1934): 29, Dorothy West Papers, MC 676 Vt-17 (box 9, f. 23), Schlesinger Library on the History of Women in America, Radcliffe Institute for Advanced Study, Harvard University.

20. James Weldon Johnson, foreword to *Challenge* 1, no. 1 (March 1934): 2, Dorothy West Papers, MC 676 Vt-17 (box 9, f. 23), Schlesinger Library on the History of Women in America, Radcliffe Institute for Advanced Study, Harvard University.

21. Dorothy West, "Dear Reader," *Challenge* 1, no. 4 (January 1936): 38, Dorothy West Papers, MC 676 Vt-17 (box 9, f. 23), Schlesinger Library on the History of Women in America, Radcliffe Institute for Advanced Study, Harvard University.

22. Dorothy West, "Dear Reader," *Challenge* 1, no. 1 (March 1934): 45, Dorothy West Papers, MC 676 Vt-17 (box 9, f. 23), Schlesinger Library on the History of Women in America, Radcliffe Institute for Advanced Study, Harvard University.

23. Mitchell and Davis, *Literary Sisters,* 150–51, 154.

24. Dorothy West, "Dear Reader," *Challenge* 2, no. 1 (Spring 1937): 40. Dorothy West Papers, MC 676 Vt-17 (box 10, f. 1). Schlesinger Library on the History of Women in America, Radcliffe Institute for Advanced Study, Harvard University.

25. West, "Dear Reader," (Spring 1937), 40.

26. Richard Wright, "Blueprint for Negro Writing," *New Challenge* 1 (Fall 1937): 53–65.

27. West, 41.

28. West, 41.

29. Sherrard-Johnson, *Dorothy West's Paradise,* 114.

30. Katrine Dalsgard, "Alive and Well and Living on the Island of Martha's Vineyard: An Interview with Dorothy West, October 29, 1988," *Langston Hughes Review* 12, no. 2 (Fall 1993): 39.

31. Unlike West, Wright sees the mingling of art and politics as easy to maintain. In "Blueprint for Negro Writing," Wright lays out the stakes of Black politics and poetics. He calls for the formation of a new literary school, one centered around his call for "Negro writers to stand shoulder

to shoulder with Negro workers in mood and outlook" (55). Having risen from the mass of Black sharecroppers in segregated Mississippi, Wright richly understood the stakes of the Communist Party's "nation within a nation" theory. For him, the function of Black writing is to both describe and affect the lives of the laboring and exploited classes of Black citizens of the United States. Implicit in Wright's essay is a form of Black cultural nationalism that is not essentialist but rather represents a collective understanding born and bred from the "plantation-feudal economy" and Jim Crow history that must be accepted so that it might be transcended. Amid national entrapment, he imagines a literary project that compels Black people living and dying under Jim Crow in the agrarian American South to see and understand their condition and assert their autonomy. See Wright, "Blueprint for Negro Writing." For more on Wright's literary transcendence alongside his editorial work with *New Challenge,* see Lawrence P. Jackson, *The Indignant Generation: A Narrative History of African American Writers and Critics, 1934–1960* (Princeton, N.J.: Princeton University Press, 2011), 71–75.

32. Laurie Champion, "Social Class Distinctions in Dorothy West's 'The Richer, the Poorer,'" *Langston Hughes Review* 16, no. 1–2 (Fall 1999–Spring 2001): 39.

33. Candice M. Jenkins, *Black Bourgeois: Class and Sex in the Flesh* (Minneapolis: University of Minnesota Press, 2019).

34. Jenkins, *Black Bourgeois,* 14.

35. Jewel Gomes, "The Wedding," *QBR: The Black Book Review* 2, no. 3 (1995): 5.

36. "Black Women Oral History Project Interview with Dorothy West, May 6, 1978," Black Women Oral History Project, Interviews, 1976–1981, "Dorothy West," OH-31, seq. 18, Schlesinger Library on the History of Women in America, Radcliffe Institute for Advanced Study, Harvard University, https://nrs.lib.harvard.edu/urn-3:rad.schl:10050463.

37. "Black Women Oral History Project Interview with Dorothy West," seq. 18.

38. "Black Women Oral History Project Interview with Dorothy West," seq. 18.

39. Sherrard-Johnson, *Dorothy West's Paradise,* 170.

40. Lionel Trilling, "Manners, Morals, and the Novel," *Kenyon Review* 10, no. 1 (Winter 1948): 11–27.

41. Trilling, "Manners, Morals, and the Novel," 18. Trilling enumerates the components of texture in an English or Continental novel: state, national name, sovereign, court, aristocracy, church, clergy, army, diplomatic service, country gentlemen, palaces, castle, manors, country houses,

parsonages, thatched cottages, ivied ruins, cathedrals, great universities, public schools, political society, sporting class, Epsom and Ascot.

42. Trilling, 19.

43. Trilling, 20.

44. Trilling, 12.

45. James W. Tuttleton, *The Novel of Manners in America* (Chapel Hill: University of North Carolina Press, 1972), xiii.

46. Tuttleton, *Novel of Manners in America*, 12.

47. Mary Sisney, "The View from the Outside: Black Novels of Manners," in *Reading and Writing Women's Lives: A Study of the Novel of Manners*, ed. Bege Bowers and Barbara Brothers (Ann Arbor: UMI Research Press, 1990), 170.

48. Verner D. Mitchell and Cynthia Davis, "Introduction: Toward a Reappraisal of Dorothy West's Work," in *Where the Wild Grape Grows: Selected Writings, 1930–1950*, by Dorothy West (Amherst: University of Massachusetts Press, 2005), 17.

49. Cheryl A. Wall, *Worrying the Line: Black Women Writers, Lineage, and Literary Tradition* (Chapel Hill: University of North Carolina Press, 2015), 13.

50. Dorothy West, *The Living Is Easy* (1948; New York: Feminist Press, 1982), 4. Future citations will appear parenthetically.

51. Tate, *Domestic Allegories of Political Desire*, 14.

52. Mary Helen Washington, *Invented Lives: Narratives of Black Women 1860–1960* (New York: Anchor Press, 1987), 350.

53. Sara Ahmed, *The Promise of Happiness* (Durham, N.C.: Duke University Press, 2010), 56.

54. Ahmed, *Promise of Happiness*, 62, 65.

55. Ahmed, 67.

56. Toni Morrison, *Sula* (New York: Knopf, 1973), 121.

57. Christina Sharpe, *In the Wake: On Blackness and Being* (Durham, N.C.: Duke University Press, 2016), 92.

58. Saidiya Hartman, *Scenes of Subjection: Terror, Slavery, and Self-Making in Nineteenth-Century America* (New York: Oxford University Press, 1997), 81.

59. Fred Moten, "The Case of Blackness," *Criticism* 50, no. 2 (Spring 2008): 187.

60. Paul L. Dunbar, "We Wear the Masks," in *Majors and Minors* (Toledo: Hadley and Hadley, 1895), 21.

61. Ann duCille, *The Coupling Convention: Sex, Text and Tradition in Black Women's Fiction* (New York: Oxford University Press, 1993), 114.

62. Hortense J. Spillers, "Mama's Baby, Papa's Maybe: An American

Grammar Book," in *Black, White, and in Color: Essays on American Literature and Culture* (Chicago: University of Chicago Press, 2013), 215.

63. Ayesha K. Hardison, *Writing through Jane Crow: Race and Gender Politics in African American Literature* (Charlottesville: University of Virginia Press, 2014), 69.

64. Mitchell and Davis, "Introduction," 37.

65. Washington, *Invented Lives*, 350.

66. Washington, 346.

67. Cathy J. Cohen, "Punks, Bulldaggers, and Welfare Queens," *GLQ: A Journal of Lesbian and Gay Studies* 3, no. 4 (May 1997): 452.

68. Cohen, "Punks, Bulldaggers, and Welfare Queens," 454.

69. For more on West's exploration of compulsive overeating, corporeality, and Black respectability politics, see Meredith Goldsmith, "The Wages of Weight: Dorothy West's Corporeal Politics," *Mosaic: An Interdisciplinary Critical Journal* 40, no. 4 (December 2007): 35–59.

70. Goldsmith, "Wages of Weight," 43.

71. Jennifer M. Wilks, "New Women and New Negroes: Archetypal Womanhood in *The Living Is Easy*," *African American Review* 39, no. 4 (Winter 2005): 569–70.

72. Amy Dru Stanley, *From Bondage to Contract: Wage Labor, Marriage, and the Market in the Age of Slave Emancipation* (New York: Cambridge University Press, 1998), 10.

73. Hartman, *Scenes of Subjection*, 125.

3. Domestic Work

1. U.S. Federal Bureau of Investigation, Document #100-104258, Alice Childress Papers, Sc MG 649 (box 1, f. 8), Schomburg Center for Research in Black Culture, Manuscripts, Archives, and Rare Books Division, New York Public Library. A copy of Alice Childress's FBI file can be accessed through her papers housed at the Schomburg Center for Research in Black Culture, Manuscripts, Archives, and Rare Books Division of the New York Public Library. Likewise, you may access a (shorter) digital version via the F. B. Eyes Digital Archive (Washington University Digital Gateway, Image Collection and Exhibitions, http://omeka.wustl.edu/omeka/exhibits /show/fbeyes) housed at Washington University in St. Louis and created in conjunction with William J. Maxwell's F.B. Eyes book project. Maxwell notes in the appendix to *F.B. Eyes: How J. Edgar Hoover's Ghostreaders Framed African American Literature* (Princeton, N.J.: Princeton University Press, 2015) that he received a paper copy of the file from scholar Mary Helen Washington in 2006. The Internet Archive maintains a duplicate

of the files housed at F.B. Eyes. Federal Bureau of Investigation, Alice
Childress FBI File, available at Internet Archive, https://archive.org
/details/AliceChildressFBIFile. I move between both versions of the file
because there are differences in what each contains.

2. Maxwell, *F.B. Eyes,* 5.

3. Maxwell, 9.

4. Mary Helen Washington, "Alice Childress, Lorraine Hansberry,
and Claudia Jones: Black Women Write the Popular Front," in *Left of the
Color Line: Race, Radicalism, and Twentieth-Century Literature of the United
States,* ed. Bill V. Mullin and James Smethurst (Chapel Hill: University of
North Carolina Press, 2003), 187.

5. U.S. Federal Bureau of Investigation memorandum of March 20,
1953, Document #100–379156, F.B. Eyes Digital Archive, http://omeka
.wustl.edu/omeka/exhibits/show/fbeyes.

6. U.S. Federal Bureau of Investigation memorandum of March 20, 1953.

7. U.S. Federal Bureau of Investigation memorandum of June 16, 1953,
Document #100-379156-1, Alice Childress Papers, Sc MG 649 (box 1, f. 8),
Schomburg Center for Research in Black Culture, Manuscripts, Archives,
and Rare Books Division, New York Public Library.

8. Simone Browne, *Dark Matters: On the Surveillance of Blackness*
(Durham, N.C.: Duke University Press, 2015), 21.

9. Browne, *Dark Matters,* 21.

10. Claudia Jones, "An End to the Neglect of the Problems of the Negro
Woman!," *PRISM: Political & Rights Issues & Social Movements* 467 (1949):
16. Likewise, Mary Helen Washington calls Childress's Mildred conversations "a virtual dramatization of the issues in Jones's essays." Washington,
"Alice Childress, Lorraine Hansberry, and Claudia Jones," 196.

11. Carole Boyce Davies, *Left of Karl Marx: The Political Life of Black
Communist Claudia Jones* (Durham, N.C.: Duke University Press,
2007), 27.

12. Michael Denning, *The Cultural Front: The Laboring of American
Culture in the Twentieth Century* (New York: Verso, 1977), 26.

13. Patricia Hill Collins, "Mammies, Matriarchs and Other Controlling
Images," in *Black Feminist Thought: Knowledge, Consciousness, and the Politics of Empowerment,* 2nd ed. (New York: Routledge, 2000), 72.

14. Kathy A. Perkins, introduction to *Selected Plays: Alice Childress,* by
Alice Childress (Evanston, Ill.: Northwestern University Press, 2011), xix.

15. Alice Childress, *Florence,* in *Selected Plays: Alice Childress,* ed. Kathy
A. Perkins (Evanston, Ill.: Northwestern University Press, 2011), 6. Future
references will appear parenthetically within the text.

16. Miriam Thaggert, *Riding Jane Crow: African American Women on the American Railroad* (Chicago: University of Illinois Press, 2022), 39.

17. Jonathan Shandell, *The American Negro Theatre and the Long Civil Rights Era* (Iowa City: University of Iowa Press, 2018), 2–3.

18. Shandell, *American Negro Theatre,* 113.

19. Washington, "Alice Childress, Lorraine Hansberry, and Claudia Jones," 183.

20. Thaggert, *Riding Jane Crow,* 23.

21. Hazel V. Carby, "The Sexual Politics of Women's Blues," in *Cultures in Babylon: Black Britain and African America* (New York: Verso, 1999), 13.

22. Frank B. Wilderson III, *Red, White, and Black: Cinema and the Structure of U.S. Antagonisms* (Durham, N.C.: Duke University Press, 2010), 5. Wilderson defines *antagonism* as "an irreconcilable struggle between entities, or positions, the resolution of which is not dialectical but entails the obliteration of one of the positions" (5).

23. Alice Childress, *Like One of the Family . . . Conversations from a Domestic's Life* (New York: Independence Publishers, 1956). Future references will appear parenthetically within the text.

24. Washington, "Alice Childress, Lorraine Hansberry, and Claudia Jones," 189–90.

25. Childress's Mildred anticipates Barbara Neely's late twentieth-century mystery-solving domestic worker, Blanche White, who shares her outspokenness and sense of autonomy. Barbara Neely, *Blanche on the Lam* (New York: Penguin Books, 1992), the first book in Neely's multibook detection series.

26. Collins, "Mammies, Matriarchs and Other Controlling Images," 69.

27. Collins, 72.

28. Trudier Harris, introduction to *Like One of the Family: Conversations from a Domestic's Life,* by Alice Childress (Boston: Beacon Press, 1986), xxxvi.

29. Trudier Harris, "'I Wish I Was a Poet': The Character as Artist in Alice Childress's *Like One of the Family,*" *Black American Literature Forum* 14, no. 1 (Spring 1980): 25.

30. Saidiya Hartman, "The Belly of the World: A Note on Black Women's Labors," *Souls: A Critical Journal of Black Politics, Culture, and Society* 19, no. 1 (January–March 2016): 171.

31. Kevin K. Gaines, *American Africans in Ghana: Black Expatriates and the Civil Rights Era* (Chapel Hill: University of North Carolina Press, 2006), 25.

32. Hughes's Simple stories revolve around the concept of a conversation

between Jesse B. Semple and Ananias Boyd, a buddy at the bar, which
allowed Hughes to craft the Black everyman's perspective regarding the
news and issues of the day. Hughes published the dialogues as part of his
"Here to Yonder" column for the *Chicago Defender* starting in February of
1943 and extending to the 1960s.

33. Davies devotes the third chapter of *Left of Karl Marx* to analyzing
the poems Jones wrote while incarcerated. These poems, along with her
journalism, constitute her as a creative writer and thus part of a more
extensive network of Black women writing in the mid-twentieth century.
William J. Maxwell makes a similar argument for employing a literary
perspective toward the journalism of Louise Thompson Patterson during
a period when African American women's writings take many nontraditional forms. William J. Maxwell, *New Negro, Old Left: African-American
Writing and Communism between the Wars* (New York: Columbia University Press, 1999), 144.

34. Mary Helen Washington, *The Other Blacklist: The African American
Literary and Cultural Left of the 1950s* (New York: Columbia University
Press, 2014), 146.

35. Robin D. G. Kelley, *Hammer and Hoe: Alabama Communists during
the Great Depression* (Chapel Hill: University of North Carolina Press,
2015), 9.

36. Claudia Jones, "On the Right to Self-Determination for the Negro
People in the Black Belt," *Political Affairs* (January 1946): 73.

37. Maxwell, *F.B. Eyes*, 16.

38. Brown, *Dark Matters*, 22.

39. Maxwell, *F.B. Eyes*, 222.

40. Jones, "End to the Neglect of the Problems of the Negro Woman!," 11.

41. "All about Miss Tubman" is not Childress's only narrativizing of the
historical figure Harriet Tubman. Childress published a play for children
about Tubman titled *When the Rattlesnake Sounds* (1975), which grew out
of a scene in her 1952 play *Gold through the Tree*. Both plays fictionalize the
time Tubman spent working as a hotel laundress in the vacation town of
Cape May, New Jersey.

42. Julia L. Mickenberg, *Learning from the Left: Children's Literature,
the Cold War, and Radical Politics in the United States* (New York: Oxford
University Press, 2005), 7.

43. Terrion L. Williamson, *Scandalize My Name: Black Feminist Practice
and the Making of Black Social Life* (Philadelphia: Temple University Press,
2016), 9.

44. Williamson, *Scandalize My Name*, 9.

45. U.S. Federal Bureau of Investigation memorandum of July 31, 1958,

Document #100-379156-26, Alice Childress Papers, Sc MG 649 (box 1, f. 8), Schomburg Center for Research in Black Culture, Manuscripts, Archives, and Rare Books Division, New York Public Library.

46. U.S. Federal Bureau of Investigation, Document #100-104258, Alice Childress Papers, Sc MG 649 (box 1, f. 8), Schomburg Center for Research in Black Culture, Manuscripts, Archives, and Rare Books Division, New York Public Library.

4. Line Work

1. Gwendolyn Brooks, *Report from Part One* (Detroit: Broadside Press, 1972), 50.

2. Brooks, *Report from Part One,* 50.

3. Brooks, 50.

4. Brooks, 193.

5. Gwendolyn Brooks, "Pete at the Zoo," in *Blacks* (Chicago: Third World Press, 1987), 361.

6. Gwendolyn Brooks, "Abruptly," in *Children Coming Home* (Chicago: David Press, 1991), 11.

7. Brooks, "Abruptly," 11.

8. Sylvia Wynter, "Unsettling the Coloniality of Being/Power/Truth /Freedom: Towards the Human, after Man, Its Overrepresentation—An Argument," *CR: The New Centennial Review* 3, no. 3 (2003): 257–337.

9. One might differentiate Brooks from other canonical writers and texts, such as Ralph Ellison's use of animal metaphors in *Invisible Man* (1952) or Zora Neale Hurston's binding of the Black and animal experiences in her ethnographic writing from *Mules and Men* (1935) or *Tell My Horse* (1938). As I have argued, Brooks moves beyond Richard Wright's employment of more traditional animal metaphors and sentimentalism in texts like *American Hunger* and *Native Son* to explore the relationship among segregation, animality, and liberation, seeking a more disruptive form of human and nonhuman affiliation. See Eve Dunbar, "Loving Gorillas: Animality, Segregation Literature, and Liberation," *American Literature* 92, no. 1 (March 2020): 123–49.

10. Frederick Douglass, *Narrative of the Life of Frederick Douglass: An American Slave* (Boston: Anti-slavery Office, 1846), 40, 45, 63.

11. Toni Morrison, *Beloved* (New York: Vintage Books, 1987), 194–95.

12. Mel Y. Chen, *Animacies: Biopolitics, Racial Mattering, and Queer Affect* (Durham, N.C.: Duke University Press, 2012), 111.

13. For more on the problematics of such yoking, see Alexander G. Weheliye, *Habeas Viscus: Racializing Assemblages, Biopolitics, and Black*

Feminist Theories of the Human (Durham, N.C.: Duke University Press, 2014); Gabriel Rosenberg, "A Race Suicide among the Hogs: The Biopolitics of Pork in the United States, 1865–1930," *American Quarterly* 68, no. 1 (2016): 53.

14. Joshua Bennett, *Being Property Once Myself: Blackness and the End of Man* (Cambridge, Mass.: Harvard University Press, 2020), 8.

15. Nicole Shukin, *Animal Capital: Rendering Life in Biopolitical Times* (Minneapolis: University of Minnesota Press, 2009), 11.

16. Cheryl A. Wall, *Worrying the Line: Black Women Writers, Lineage, and Literary Tradition* (Chapel Hill: University of North Carolina Press, 2005), 8.

17. Wall, *Worrying the Line,* 8–12.

18. See Eve Dunbar, "Loving Gorillas: Segregation Literature, Animality, and Black Liberation," *American Literature* 92, no. 1 (March 2020): 123–49.

19. Richard Wright, *Native Son* (New York: Harper & Brothers, 1940), 233.

20. Wright, *Native Son,* 229.

21. Wright, 338–39. See also Richard Wright, "How 'Bigger' Was Born," *Saturday Review of Literature* 22, no. 6 (June 1, 1940): 3–4, 17–20. Richard Wright based some of the events in *Native Son* on the case of Robert Nixon, who was accused, tried, and executed for the 1938 murder of Florence Johnson. For a more detailed exploration of the Robert Nixon case, see Elizabeth Dale, *Robert Nixon and Police Torture: In Chicago, 1871–1971* (Dekalb: Northern Illinois University Press, 2016).

22. Wright, *Native Son,* 342, 344.

23. Matthew Lambert suggests that Wright's use of the rat in *Native Son* allows Bigger to take on "a kind of rat-ness that transforms him into a subject of critical empathy rather than an object of pity or fear." Matthew Lambert, "'That Sonofabitch Could Cut Your Throat': Bigger and the Black Rat in Richard Wright's *Native Son,*" *Journal of the Midwest Modern Language Association* 49, no. 1 (Spring 2016): 81. My argument differs from Lambert's in that I'm less interested in the ways the animal becomes a way of humanizing Black characters than in the ways it becomes a mode of redefining and crafting another genre of human.

24. See chapter entitled "Rat" in Bennett, *Being Property Once Myself.* Bennett offers an extensive reading of the precarity of Black life in Richard Wright's work as mediated through Wright's animal metaphors.

25. Michael Lunblad, "From Animal to Animality Studies," *PMLA* 124, no. 2 (2009): 497.

26. See Donna Haraway, *Simians, Cyborgs, and Women: The Reinvention of Nature* (New York: Routledge, 1991); Katherine N. Hayles, *How We Became Posthuman: Virtual Bodies in Cybernetics, Literature, and Informatics* (Chicago: University of Chicago Press, 1999); Cary Wolfe, *Animal Rites: American Culture, the Discourses of Species, and Posthumanist Theory* (Chicago: University of Chicago Press, 2003); Mel Y. Chen, *Animacies: Biopolitics, Racial Mattering, and Queer Affect* (Durham, N.C.: Duke University Press, 2021); Rosi Braidotti, *The Posthuman* (Malden, Mass.: Polity, 2013), Richard Grusin, ed., *The Nonhuman Turn* (Minneapolis: University of Minnesota Press, 2015); Kristen Lillvis, *Posthuman Blackness and the Black Female Imagination* (Athens: University of Georgia Press, 2017).

27. Zakiyyah Iman Jackson, "Review: Animal: New Directions in the Theorization of Race and Posthumanism," *Feminist Studies* 39, no. 3 (2013): 670.

28. Sylvia Wynter, "Unsettling the Coloniality of Being/Power/Truth /Freedom: Towards the Human, after Man, Its Overrepresentation— An Argument," *CR: The New Centennial Review* 3, no. 3 (Fall 2003): 260; Weheliye, *Habeas Viscus*, 4.

29. Sylvia Wynter, "On How We Mistook the Map for the Territory, and Reimprisoned Ourselves in Our Unbearable Wrongness of Being, of *Desêtre*: Black Studies toward the Human Project," in *A Companion to African-American Studies*, ed. Jane Gordon and Lewis Gordon (London: Blackwell, 2007), 112.

30. See Mary Helen Washington, "'Taming All That Anger Down': Race and Silence in Gwendolyn Brooks' *Maud Martha*," *Massachusetts Review* 24, no. 4 (Summer 1983); Valerie Frazier, "Domestic Epic Warfare in *Maud Martha*," *African American Review* 39, no. 1 (Spring/Summer 2005); Kevin Quashie, *The Sovereignty of Quiet: Beyond Resistance in Black Culture* (New Brunswick, N.J.: Rutgers University Press, 2012); Megan K. Ahern, "Creative Multivalence: Social Engagement beyond Naturalism in Gwendolyn Brooks's *Maud Martha*," *African American Review* 47, no. 2–3 (2014).

31. Hortense J. Spillers, "'All the Things You Could Be by Now, If Sigmund Freud's Wife Was Your Mother': Psychoanalysis and Race," in *Black, White, and In Color: Essays on American Literature and Culture* (Chicago: University of Chicago Press, 2003), 136.

32. Quashie, *Sovereignty of Quiet*, 52.

33. Gwendolyn Brooks, *Maud Martha* (1953; Chicago: Third World Press, 1993), 163. Future citations will appear parenthetically.

34. Malin Lavon Walther, "Re-Wrighting *Native Son*: Gwendolyn

Brooks's Domestic Aesthetic in *Maud Martha*," *Tulsa Studies in Women's Literature* 13, no. 1 (1994): 143.

35. Frazier, "Domestic Epic Warfare in *Maud Martha*," 137.

36. Frazier, 143.

37. Ahern, "Creative Multivalence," 318.

38. Ahern, 319.

39. Michael Foucault, "Right of Death and Power over Life," *Biopolitics: A Reader*, ed. Timothy Campbell and Adam Sitze (Durham, N.C.: Duke University Press, 2013).

40. Kevin Quashie argues in his reading of *Maud Martha* that the existentialist dynamic of the text seeps into its very structure, which is episodic and anecdotal rather than consequential. Quashie, *Sovereignty of Quiet*, 53.

41. Thomas Jefferson, *Notes on the State of Virginia*, 2nd American ed. (Philadelphia: Printed for Mathew Carey, no. 118, Market-Street November 12, 1794), 201.

42. Wright, *Native Son*, 33.

43. Badia Sahar Ahad, *Freud Upside Down: African American Literature and Psychoanalytic Culture* (Chicago: University of Illinois Press, 2010), 5.

44. Ahad, *Freud Upside Down*, 5.

45. Anne Anlin Cheng, *The Melancholy of Race* (New York: Oxford University Press, 2000), 3–7.

46. Cheng, *Melancholy of Race*, 28.

47. Spillers, "'All the Things You Could Be by Now,'" 385.

48. Sigmund Freud, *The Uncanny*, trans. David McLintock (1919; London: Penguin Books, 2003), 123.

49. Freud, *Uncanny*, 124.

50. Spillers, "'All the Things You Could Be by Now,'" 400.

51. Monique Wittig, "The Straight Mind," in *The Straight Mind and Other Essays* (Boston: Beacon Press, 1992).

52. Quashie, *Sovereignty of Quiet*, 52.

53. Stephen Best and Sharon Marcus, "Surface Reading: An Introduction," *Representations* 101, no. 1 (November 2009): 1–21.

54. Lloyd Pratt, *The Strangers Book: The Human of African American Literature* (Philadelphia: University of Pennsylvania, 2016), 10.

55. Frazier, "Domestic Epic Warfare in *Maud Martha*," 133.

56. Washington, "'Taming All That Anger Down,'" 457.

57. Washington, 463.

58. Psyche A. Williams-Forson, *Building Houses out of Chicken Legs: Black Women, Food and Power* (Chapel Hill: University of North Carolina Press, 2006), 27.

59. Williams-Forson, *Building Houses out of Chicken Legs,* 1.

60. Quashie, *Sovereignty of Quiet,* 45.

61. Frazier, "Domestic Epic Warfare in *Maud Martha,*" 139.

62. Sharon Holland, Marcia Ochoa, and Kyla Wazana Tompkins, "Introduction: On the Visceral," *GLQ: Journal of Lesbian and Gay Studies* 20, no. 4 (October 2014): 394.

63. Walter Benjamin, "One-Way Street," in *Reflections: Essays, Aphorisms, Autobiographical Writings* (New York: Schocken Books, 1986), 66.

64. Elspeth Probyn, *Carnal Appetites: Food, Sex, Identities* (New York: Routledge, 2000), 139.

65. Mary Douglas, *Purity and Danger: An Analysis of the Concept of Pollution and Taboo* (New York: Routledge, 1966). Mary Douglas suggests in her canonical anthropological study on social contamination that social marginality and ambiguity create fear and danger in the social consciousness. "There is danger in this ambiguity," according to Douglas, because "the polluting person is always in the wrong. He has developed some wrong condition or simply crossed some line which should not have been crossed and this displacement unleashes danger for someone" (140). Kin to this understanding of contamination, then, is the notion that purity is socially preferred because it entails the unambiguous maintenance of order. In this sense, then, Maud Martha has allowed the impurity to permeate the narrative. See Maggie Kilgour, *Communion to Cannibalism: An Anatomy of Metaphors of Incorporation* (Princeton, N.J.: Princeton University Press, 1990).

66. Nicole R. Fleetwood, *Troubling Vision: Performance, Visuality, and Blackness* (Chicago: University of Chicago Press, 2011).

67. Kyla Wazana Tompkins, *Racial Indigestion: Eating Bodies in the 19th Century* (New York: New York University Press, 2012), 11.

68. "Farm Family Enlists to Produce Food for the War Effort," *Chicago Defender,* January 23, 1943.

69. "Patriotic Meal Planner Must Use Less Meat," *Chicago Defender,* October 31, 1942; "Sugarless Cake Recipe Solve Menu Problem," *Chicago Defender,* March 14, 1942; "It's All Right If You Have Sugar to Spare," *Chicago Defender,* October 24, 1942; "Dairy Cook's Corner by Alice Andrews," *Chicago Defender,* March 6, 1943.

70. "New OPA Order to Place Negroes on Ration Boards," *Chicago Defender,* May 29, 1943. This OPA order is particularly essential because board representation gave women and Black people access to price control information, which was of particular concern to *Defender* readers. These readers were worried that Black consumers, especially Southern consumers, were subject to price differentials levied against residents of Black

neighborhoods, price speculation and overcharging for rationed commodities, and unequal rationing quotas given to Blacks by local and state rationing boards.

71. While I'm genuinely interested in contemporary critiques of the exploitation of human and nonhuman animals by agribusiness and the factory farm industry, Brooks's narrative exists outside these critiques (e.g., of large-scale poultry production) as we have come to know them in the late twentieth and early twenty-first centuries. It wasn't until World War II that poultry became a viable agricultural pursuit for large farms. Before the rationing of beef and the introduction of chicken as a sustainable protein substitute for red meat by the Office of Price Administration in 1943, most poultry-raising was small-scale and carried out by women. Poultry was notoriously susceptible to disease, which made their husbandry of little interest to male-dominated large-scale farms. This would change after WWII with the introduction of a national appetite for chicken and the growth of industrialized chicken farms and poultry processing plants throughout the American South. For more on the history of the connection between the rise of the poultry industry and Black women's labor, see LaGuana Gray, *We Just Keep Running the Line: Black Southern Women and the Poultry Processing Industry* (Baton Rouge: Louisiana State University Press, 2014).

72. Ahern defines *multivalence* as the ability of the text to simultaneously express "multiple, even conflicting, sentiments, without necessarily specifying the truth-value of any one of them." Ahern, "Creative Multivalence," 318.

73. Barbara Johnson, "Apostrophe, Animation, and Abortion," *Diacritics* 16, no. 1 (Spring 1986): 32.

74. Gwendolyn Brooks, "The Mother," in *Blacks* (Chicago: Third World Press, 1987), 21.

75. Jonathan Culler, "Apostrophe," *Diacritics* 7, no. 4 (December 1977): 59.

76. Culler, "Apostrophe," 62. It is important to note that Culler is arguing against interpreting direct address to an object as the poet's address to the "divine" or some other sort of heavenly spirit. Culler reads the address as more secular and material, which substantiates the object's transition to subject status.

77. Culler, 63.

78. Brooks, *Report from Part One*, 175.

79. I want to thank Richard Menke for drawing my attention to this potential allusion. For more on Diogenes of Sinope see Diogenes Laërtius, *Lives and Opinions of Eminent Philosophers*, trans. C. D. Younge (London: Bell and Sons, 1915), 231.

80. Ayesha K. Hardison, *Writing through Jane Crow* (Charlottesville: University of Virginia Press, 2014), 162.

81. Here I am using Maggie Kilgour's sense of incorporation, which she describes as the act in which "an external object is taken inside another." For Kilgour, incorporation "depends upon and enforces an absolute division between inside and outside," but the act of incorporation appears to dissolve. Kilgour, *From Communion to Cannibalism*, 4.

82. bell hooks, "Eating the Other: Desire and Resistance," in *Black Looks: Race and Representation* (Boston: South End Press, 1992), 36.

83. Wolfe, *Animal Rites*, 2.

84. Carol Adams, *The Sexual Politics of Meat: A Feminist-Vegetarian Critical Theory* (New York: Continuum, 1990), 45.

85. Brooks, *Report from Part One*, 171.

86. Barbara Christian, *Black Feminist Criticism: Perspectives on Black Women Writers*, 4th ed. (New York: Pergamon, 1989), 176.

Coda

1. Joan Entmacher, Katherine Gallagher Robbins, Julie Bogtman, and Lauren Frohlich, "Insecure & Unequal: Poverty and Income among Women and Families 2000–2012," National Women's Law Center, 2013, https://nwlc.org/wp-content/uploads/2015/08/nwlc_2012_povertyreport.pdf. See also Nazgol Ghandnoosh, Emma Stammen, and Kevin Muhitch, "Fact Sheet: Parents in Prison," Sentencing Project, November 17, 2021, https://www.sentencingproject.org/policy-brief/parents-in-prison/.

2. "When Men Murder Women: An Analysis of 2012 Homicide Data," Violence Policy Center, 2014, 4–5, http://www.vpc.org/studies/wmmw2014.pdf.

3. Julius B. Fleming Jr., *Black Patience: Performance, Civil Rights, and the Unfinished Project of Emancipation* (New York: New York University Press, 2022), 6.

4. The George Floyd Justice in Policing Act of 2021 is a bipartisan bill out of the U.S. House of Representatives that holds law enforcement accountable for misconduct, restricts dangerous policing practices, calls for data collection on misconduct, and establishes best practices and training requirements. See George Floyd Justice in Policing Act of 2021, H.R. 1280, 117th Cong. (2021–2022), https://www.congress.gov/bill/117th-congress/house-bill/1280/text.

5. Miles Pope, "Amy Sherald on Making Breonna Taylor's Portrait," *Vanity Fair*, September 2020, https://www.vanityfair.com/culture/2020/08/amy-sherald-on-making-breonna-taylors-cover-portrait.

6. Makeda Easter, "How Amy Sherald's Paintings Capture the Spectacularly Mundane Moments of Black Life," *Los Angeles Times,* March 31, 2021, https://www.latimes.com/entertainment-arts/story/2021-03-31/amy-sherald-profile-hauser-wirth-los-angeles.

7. Pope, "Amy Sherald on Making Breonna Taylor's Portrait."

8. Pope.

9. Ta-Nehisi Coates, "The Life Breonna Taylor Lived, in the Words of Her Mother," *Vanity Fair,* September 2020, https://www.vanityfair.com/culture/2020/08/breonna-taylor.

Index

Page numbers in italics indicate photographs and other illustrations.

capitalism, 29, 31–35, 81, 120
Capshaw, Katharine, 43, 160n55
captive flesh: definition of, 160n66
Carby, Hazel V., 32, 92
Challenge/New Challenge magazines, 20, 59, 60–67, 79. *See also* West, Dorothy
Champion, Laurie: on West's novels, 64
Chen, Mel Y., 114
Cheng, Anne Anlin: on doll tests, 124
Chicago: artistic renaissance in, 17
children and young adult fiction: Petry's, 28–29, 41–42, 43. See also *Harriet Tubman: Conductor on the Underground Railroad* (novel, Petry); *Tituba of Salem Village* (novel, Petry)
Childress, Alice, 3, 21; Communist Party/Left associations, 18, 87–88, 92, 97, 101; "Conversations from Life," 87, 95–96; FBI file on, 21, 87–91, 90, 92, 100, 103, 104, 109–10; *Gold through the Tree*, 168n41; monstrous turns in works of, 11, 95; on satisfaction, 8; segregation-era writing, 4–5; *When the Rattlesnake Sounds*, 168n41. See also *Florence* (play, Childress); *Like One of the Family: Conversations from a Domestic's Life* (short stories, Childress)
Christian, Barbara: on *Maud Martha*, 141
Christopher, Mary (pseudonym). *See* West, Dorothy
citizenship, U.S., 43, 119, 143; entitlement of Blacks to, 3, 124, 127, 140; exclusion of Blacks from full, 25, 57
civil rights, 48, 70, 84, 138; struggles for, 43, 66. See also *Brown v. Board of Education of Topeka* (1954); desegregation; integration
Civil Rights Act of 1964, 42
Clark, Keith, 157n20; on *The Street*, 32
Clark, Kenneth and Mamie: doll tests conducted by, 124
class, 19, 24, 36, 66, 78, 102; differentiation among, 65, 67, 69–70;

expectations based on, 72–73; privilege of, 64, 65, 69. *See also* Blacks: middle-class; Blacks: working-class; Black womanhood/women: middle-class; Black womanhood/women: working-class
Coates, Ta-Nehisi, 145
Cohen, Cathy J., 38, 79–80
Collins, Patricia Hill: on *Like One of the Family*, 96
color, 36, 78; people of, 24, 119, 140, 156n10. *See also* race
color line, 91, 92, 94, 95, 115
Communist Party: Black Belt thesis of, 61; Childress's associations with, 18, 87–88, 91, 92; on gender egalitarianism, 155n48; influence on Black literary and cultural production, 17–18, 63, 90–91, 143; *Like One of the Family* reflecting ideas of, 102–3; members reading Black authors, 87, 109; nation within a nation theory, 162–63n31
completeness, 3, 100. *See also* wholeness
contentment, 7, 143. *See also* happiness; joy; satisfaction, Black
Cottom, Tressie McMillan, 29, 31, 33
counterveillance. *See* dark sousveillance; surveillance
courtship: West's ideas on, 56, 57. *See also* marriage(s); romance
Cullen, Countee: published in *Challenge* magazine, 61
Culler, Jonathan, 136–37, 174n76
culture, 8, 25, 27, 67, 79, 116; Black, 14, 33, 68

dark sousveillance, 21, 89, 103. *See also* Childress, Alice: FBI file on; surveillance
Davies, Carole Boyce: on Claudia Jones, 17–18; *Left of Karl Marx*, 168n33
Davis, Angela Y., 16, 17, 18

Fauset, Jessie: *Brownies' Book* series, 160n55

femininity, 59, 77, 130. *See also* gender

feminism/feminists, Black, 17, 70, 127; critique of family and nation by, 84–85; killjoy figure, 72, 79; scholarship of, 7–8, 66; understanding of women's joy and wholeness, 6–7

Fleetwood, Nicole R.: troubling vision concept, 133

Fleming, Julius B., Jr., 144

Florence (play, Childress), 20–21, 88, 91–95, 97, 102

Floyd, George: murder of, 145

Foley, Barbara, 16, 155n48

Frazier, E. Franklin: *The Negro Family in the United States,* 58–59

Frazier, Valerie: on *Maud Martha,* 121–22, 129, 130

freedom, 5, 8, 17, 103, 130; for Black women, 20, 91, 92, 144; desires for, 16, 128. *See also* autonomy; emancipation, Black; liberation, Black; mobility

Freedom newspaper, 44, 87, 95, 96, 108. *See also* Robeson, Paul

Freud, Sigmund, 128; "Mourning and Melancholia," 124, 125

fugitivity, 16, 24, 40–41, 111

Gaines, Kevin K., 100

Garvey, Marcus, 16

gaze: external, 9–10; white, 40, 107, 119, 128

gender, 29, 37, 38, 91, 119, 144, 155n48; analyzing women's struggles through, 17–18; analyzing workers' struggles through, 91; egalitarianism of, 155n48; expectations based on, 14, 67, 70, 72–73; *The Living Is Easy* critiques of, 66, 73; race and, 70, 154n36; roles of, 71, 139; systemic inequities of, 3, 35. *See also* femininity; masculinity; ungendering

George Floyd Justice in Policing Act of 2021, 145, 175n4

Goldsmith, Meredith: on *The Living Is Easy,* 80

gothic genre, 12–13, 36, 157n10

Gray, Freddie: murder of, 145

Great Migration, 37. *See also* migration narratives

Green, Tara T., 7

Griffin, Farah Jasmine: on *The Street,* 27

Hansberry, Lorraine: FBI file on, 87

happiness, 3, 32, 59, 70–72. *See also* contentment; joy; satisfaction, Black

Hardison, Ayesha K.: on *The Living Is Easy,* 78; on *Maud Martha,* 139

Harlem, 23, 31, 33–40, 42, 88, 92, 108

Harlem Renaissance, 17, 56, 60

Harriet Tubman (Darby, wood engraving on paper), 46

Harriet Tubman: Conductor on the Underground Railroad (novel, Petry), 20, 24, 42, 44–45, 47–49, 50, 53, 105. *See also* Petry, Ann

Harris, LaShawn, 37

Harris, Trudier: on *Like One of the Family,* 96, 98; on *The Street,* 34

Hartman, Saidiya, 37, 38, 58, 75, 83, 99

Henderson, Carol E.: on *The Street,* 36

heteronormativity. *See* families/family: heteronormative; marriages: heteronormative

heterosexuality, 40, 56, 80. *See also* homosexuality

hierarchies, 113, 139; disruption of established, 132, 136; Enlightenment, 14–15; racial, 43, 116, 117, 128

Higashida, Cheryl, 16, 18

home: as radical site of national disruption, 20; as space of joy, 140–41. *See also* domesticity; families/family

home work, 55–85; Black Left and, 60–67; discourses of seduction,

women subjected to, 10, 83. *See also*
bigotry; exclusion, Black; Jim Crow
era; racism; segregation
wholeness, 2, 4, 6–8. *See also*
completeness
Wilderson, Frank B., III, 94; definition
of antagonism, 167n22
Wilks, Jennifer M.: on *The Living Is
Easy*, 80–81
Williams-Forson, Psyche A.: on Black
women's use of chickens, 130
Williamson, Terrion L., 106
Wilson, Harriet E., 50; *Our Nig*, 26,
156n10
witchcraft. *See* Salem witch trials
Wittig, Monique: on *Maud Martha*,
126
women. *See* Black midcentury women

writers; Black womanhood/
women; femininity; feminism/
feminists, Black
work. *See* domestic work/workers,
Black; radical work; ugly work
Wright, Richard, 67, 131; animal sym-
bolism used by, 115–17, 118, 169n9;
Black Boy, 115, 116–17; "Blueprint
for Negro Writing," 63, 162–63n31;
Communist Party association,
63; *Native Son*, 26–27, 115–16, 121,
123–24, 170n21, 170n23; published
in *New Challenge* magazine, 62,
63, 64
Wynter, Sylvia, 14–15, 18, 112, 117–18

young adult fiction. *See* children and
young adult fiction

Eve Dunbar is professor of English, holding the Jean Webster Chair at Vassar College. She is author of *Black Regions of the Imagination: African American Writers between the Nation and the World* and coeditor of *African American Literature in Transition, 1930–1940.*